I0646330

Henry M. Field

Gibraltar

Henry M. Field

Gibraltar

ISBN/EAN: 9783743347953

Manufactured in Europe, USA, Canada, Australia, Japa

Cover: Foto ©ninafisch / pixelio.de

Manufactured and distributed by brebook publishing software (www.brebook.com)

Henry M. Field

Gibraltar

BY

HENRY M. FIELD

ILLUSTRATED

LONDON: CHAPMAN AND HALL, LIMITED.

1889.

[All rights reserved.]

TROW'S
PRINTING AND BOOKBINDING COMPANY,
NEW YORK.

To My Friend and Neighbor

IN THE BERKSHIRE HILLS,

JOSEPH H. CHOATE,

WHO FINDS IT A RELIEF NOW AND THEN
TO TURN FROM THE HARD LABORS OF THE LAW
TO THE ROMANCE OF TRAVEL:
I SEND AS A CHRISTMAS PRESENT
A STORY OF FORTRESS AND SIEGE
THAT MAY BEGUILE A VACANT HOUR
AS HE SITS BEFORE HIS WINTER EVENING FIRE.

PREFACE.

THE common tour in Spain does not include Gibraltar. Indeed it is not a part of Spain, for, though connected with the Spanish Peninsula, it belongs to England; and to one who likes to preserve a unity in his memories of a country and people, this modern fortress, with its English garrison, is not "in color" with the old picturesque kingdom of the Goths and Moors. Nor is it on the great lines of travel. It is not touched by any railroad, and by steamers only at intervals of days, so that it has come to be known as a place which it is at once difficult to get to and to get away from. Hence easy-going travellers, who are content to take circular tickets and follow fixed routes, give Gibraltar the go-by, though by so doing they miss a place that is unique in the world—unique in position, in picturesqueness, and in history. That mighty Rock, "standing out of the water and in the water," (as on the day when the old world perished;) is one of the Pillars of Hercules, that once marked the very end of the world; and around its base ancient and modern history flow together, as the waters of the Atlantic mingle with those of the Mediterranean. Like Constantinople, it is throned on two seas and two continents. As Europe at its southeastern corner stands face to face with Asia; at its southwestern it is face to face with Africa: and these were the two points of the Moslem invasion. But here the natural course of history was reversed, as that invasion began in the West. Hundreds of years before the Turk crossed the Bosphorus, the Moor crossed the Straits of Gibraltar. His coming was the signal of an endless war of races and religions, whose lurid flames lighted up the dark background of the stormy coast. The Rock, which was the "storm-centre" of all those clouds of war, is surely worth the attention of the passing traveller. That it has been so long neglected, is the sufficient reason for an attempt to make it better known.

CONTENTS.

LIST OF ILLUSTRATIONS.

CHAPTER I.

I HEARD the last gun of the Old Year fired from the top of the Rock, and the first gun of the New. It was the very last day of 1886 that we entered the Straits of Gibraltar. The sea was smooth, the sky was clear, and the atmosphere so warm and bright that it seemed as if winter had changed places with summer, and that in December we were breathing the air of June.

On a day like this, when the sea is calm and still, groups of travellers sit about on the deck, watching the shores on either hand. How near they come to each other, only nine miles dividing the most southern point of Europe from the most northern point of Africa! Perhaps they once came together, forming a mountain chain which separated the sea from the ocean. But since the barrier was burst, the waters have rushed through with resistless power. Looking over the side of the ship, we observe that the current is setting eastward, which would not excite surprise were it not that it never turns back. The Mediterranean is a tideless sea: it does not ebb and flow, but pours its mighty volume ceaselessly in the same

direction. This, the geographers tell us, is a provision of
nature to supply the waste caused by the greater evapora-
tion at the eastern end of the Great Sea. But this satis-
fies us only in part, since while this current flows on the
surface, there is another, though perhaps a feebler, current flowing in the opposite direction. Down hundreds
of fathoms deep, a hidden Gulf Stream is pouring back
into the bosom of the ocean. This system of the ocean
currents is one of the mysteries which we do not fully
understand. It seems as if there were a spirit moving
not only upon the waters, but in the waters; as if the
great deep were a living organism, of which the ebb and
flow were like the circulation of the blood in the human
frame. Or shall we say that this upper current represents
the Stream of Life, which might seem to be over-full
were it not that far down in the depths the excess of Life
is relieved by the black waters of Death that are flowing
darkly beneath?

Turning from the sea to the shore, on our left is Tarifa,
the most southern point of Spain and of Europe—a point
far more picturesque than the low, wooded spit of land
that forms the most southern point of Asia, which the
"globe-trotter" rounds as he comes into the harbor of
Singapore, for here the headland that juts into the sea is
crowned by a Moorish castle, on the ramparts of which,
in the good old times of the Barbary pirates, sentinels
kept watch of ships that should attempt to pass the
Straits from either direction: for incomers and outgoers

alike had to lower their flags, and pay tribute to those who counted themselves the rightful lords of this whole watery realm. I wonder that the Free-Traders do not ring the changes on the fact that the very word *tariff* is derived from this ancient stronghold, at which the mariners of the Middle Ages paid "duties" to the robbers of the sea. If both sides of the Straits of Gibraltar were to-day, as they once were, under the control of the same Moslem power, we might have two castles—one in Europe and one in Africa—like the "Castles of Europe and Asia," that still guard the Dardanelles, at which all ships of commerce are required to stop and report before they can pass; while ships-of-war carrying too many guns, cannot pass at all without special permission from Constantinople.

But the days of the sea-robbers are ended, and the Mediterranean is free to all the commerce of the world The Castle of Tarifa is still kept up, and makes a picturesque object on the Spanish coast, but no corsair watches the approach of the distant sail, and no gun checks her speed; every ship—English, French, or Spanish—passes unmolested on her way between these peaceful shores. Instead of the mutual hatred which once existed between the two sides of the Straits, they are in friendly intercourse, and to-day, under these smiling skies, Spain looks love to Barbary, and Barbary to Spain.

While thus turning our eyes landward and seaward, we have been rounding into a bay, and coming in sight of a mighty rock that looms up grandly before us. Although

it was but the middle of the afternoon, the winter sun
hung low, and striking across the bay outlined against the
sky the figure of a lion couchant—a true British lion, not
unlike those in Trafalgar Square in London, only that the
bronze is changed to stone, and the figure carved out of a
mountain! But the lion is there, with his kingly head
turned toward Spain, as if in defiance of his former master, every feature bearing the character of leonine majesty
and power. That is Gibraltar!

It is a common saying that "some men achieve greatness, and some have greatness thrust upon them." The
same may be said of places; but here is one to which both
descriptions may be applied—that has had greatness
thrust upon it by nature, and has achieved it in history.
There is not a more picturesque spot in Europe. The Rock
is fourteen hundred feet high—more than three times as
high as Edinburgh Castle, and not, like that, firm-set upon the solid ground, but rising out of the seas—and girdled
with the strongest fortifications in the world. Such greatness has nature thrust upon Gibraltar. And few places
have seen more history, as few have been fought over
more times than this in the long wars of the Spaniard and
the Moor; for here the Moor first set foot in Europe, and
gave name to the place (Gibraltar being merely Gebel-el-
Tarik, the mountain of Tarik, the Moorish invader), and
here departed from it, after a conflict of nearly eight hundred years.

The steamer anchors in the bay, half a mile from shore,

THE LION COUCHANT.

and a boat takes us off to the quay, where after being duly
registered by the police, we are permitted to pass under
the massive arches, and through the heavy gates
double line of fortifications, and enter Waterport . .
the one and almost only street of Gibraltar, where we
quarters in that most comfortable refuge of the travel.
the Royal Hotel, which, for the period of our stay, is t.
be our home.

When I stepped on shore I was among strangers: even
the friend who had been my companion through Spain
had remained in Cadiz, since in coming under the Englia
flag I had no longer need of a Spanish interpreter, and I
felt a little lonely; for inside these walls there was not a
human being, man or woman, whom I had ever seen before. Yet one who has been knocked about the world as I
have been, soon makes himself at home, and in an hour I
had found, if not a familiar face, at least a familiar name,
which gave me a right to claim acquaintance. Readers
whose memories run back thirty years to the laying of
the first Atlantic Cable in 1858, may recall the fact that
the messages from Newfoundland were signed by an
operator who bore the singular name of De Santy, and
when the pulse of the old sea-cord grew faint and flut-
tering, as if it were muttering incoherent phrases before it
drew its last breath, we were accustomed to receive daily
messages signed "All right: De Santy!" which kept up
our courage for a time, until we found that "All right"
was "All wrong." The circumstance afforded much

amusement at the time, and Dr. Holmes wrote one of his wittiest poems about it, in which the refrain of every verse was "All right: De Sauty!" Well, the message was true, at least in one sense, for De Sauty was all right, if the cable was not. The cable died, but the stout-hearted operator lived, and is at this moment the manager of the Eastern Telegraph Company in Gibraltar. This is one of those great English companies, which have their centre in London, and whose "lines have" literally "gone out through all the earth." Its "home field" is the Mediterranean, from which it reaches out long arms down the Red Sea to India and Australia, and indeed to all the Eastern world. Its General Manager is Sir James Anderson, who commanded the Great Eastern when she laid the cable successfully in 1866. I had crossed the ocean with him in '67, and now, wishing to do me a good turn, he had insisted on my taking a letter to all their offices on both sides of the Mediterranean, to transmit my messages free! This was a pretty big license; his letter was almost like one of Paul's epistles "to the twelve tribes scattered abroad, greeting." It contained a sort of general direction to make myself at home in all creation!

With such an introduction I felt at home in the telegraph office in Gibraltar, and especially when I could take by the hand our old friend De Sauty. He has a hearty grip, which speaks for the true Englishman that he is. If any of my countrymen had supposed that he died with the cable, I am happy to say that he not only "still lives," but is very much alive. He at once sent off to London a message to my friends in America—a good-bye for the old year, which brought me the next morning a greeting for the new.

From the telegraph office I took my way to that of the American Consul, who gave me a welcome such as I could find in no other house in Gibraltar, since his is the only American family! When I asked after my countrymen (who, as they are going up and down in the earth, and show themselves everywhere, I took for granted must be here), he answered that there was "not one!" He is not only the official representative of our country, but he and his children the only Americans. This being so, it is a happy circumstance that the Great Republic is so well represented; for a better man than Horatio J. Sprague could not be found in the two hemispheres. He is the oldest Consul in the service, having been forty years at this post, where his father, who was appointed by General Jackson, was Consul before him. He received *his* appointment from President Polk. Through all these years he has maintained the honor of the American name, and to-day there is not within the walls of Gibraltar a man—soldier or civilian—who is more respected than this solitary representative of our country.

Some may think there is not much need of a Consul where there are no Americans, and yet nearly five hundred ships sailed from this port last year for America: pity that he should have to confess that very few bore the

American flag! Thus the post is a responsible one, and at times involves duties the most delicate and difficult, as in the late war, when the Sumter was lying here, with three or four American ships off the harbor (for they were not permitted to remain in port but twenty-four hours) to prevent her escape. At that time the Consul was constantly on the watch, only to see the privateer get off at last by the transparent device of taking out her guns, and being sold to an English owner, who immediately hoisted the English flag, and put to sea in broad daylight in the face of our ships, and made her way to Liverpool, where she was fitted out as a blockade-runner!

Those were trying days for expatriated Americans. However, it was all made up when Peace came, and Peace with Victory—with the Union restored and the country saved. Since then it has been the privilege of the Consul at Gibraltar to welcome many who took part in the great struggle, among them Generals Grant and Sherman and Admiral Farragut. Of course a soldier is always interested in a fortress, for it is in the line of his profession; and the greatest fortification in the world could but be regarded with a curious eye by old soldiers like those who had led our armies for four years; who had conducted great campaigns, with long marches and battles and sieges—battles among the bloodiest of modern times, and one siege (that of Richmond) which lasted as long as the famous siege of Gibraltar.

But perhaps no one felt a keener interest in what he

saw here than the old sea-dog, who had bombarded the forts at the mouth of the Mississippi six days and nights; had broken the heavy iron boom stretched across the river; and run his ships past the forts under a tremendous fire; only to find still before him a fleet greater than his own, of twenty armed steamers, four ironclad rams, and a multitude of fire-rafts, all of which he attacked and destroyed, and captured New Orleans, an achievement in naval warfare as great as any ever wrought by Nelson. To Farragut Gibraltar was nothing more than a big ship, whose decks were ramparts. Pretty long decks they were, to be sure, but only furnishing so many more port-holes, and carrying so many more guns, and enabling its commander to fire a more tremendous broadside.

Talking over these things fired my patriotic breast till I began to feel as if I were in "mine ain countrie," and among my American kinsmen. And as I walked from the Consul's back to the Royal Hotel, I did not feel quite so lonely in Gibraltar as I felt an hour before.

As the afternoon wore away, the Spaniards who had come in from the country to market, to buy or sell, began to disappear, and soon went hurrying out, while the belated townsmen came hurrying in. At half-past five the evening gun from the top of the Rock boomed over land and sea, and with a few minutes' grace for the last straggler, the gates of the double line of fortifications were closed for the night, and there was no more going out or coming in till morning. It gave me a little uncomfortable feeling to be thus imprisoned in a fortress, with no possibility of escape. The bustling streets soon subsided into quietness. At half-past nine another gun was the signal for the soldiers to return to their barracks; and soon the town was as tranquil as a New England village. As I stepped out upon the balcony, the stillness seemed almost unnatural. I heard no cry of " All's well " from the sentinel pacing the ramparts, as from sailors on the deck, nor the " Ave Maria santissima " of the Spanish watchman. Not even the howling of a dog broke the stillness of the night. The moon, but in her second quarter, did not shut out the light of stars, which were shining brightly on Rock and Bay. Even the heavy black guns looked peaceful in the soft and tender light. It was the last night of the year—and therefore a holy night, as it was to be marked by a Holy Nativity—the birth of a New Year, a " holy child," as it would come from the hands of God unstained by sin. A little before midnight I fell asleep, from which I started up at the sound of the morning gun. The Old Year was dead! He had been a long time dying, but there is always a shock when the end comes. And yet in that same midnight a new star appeared in the East, bringing fresh hope to the poor old world. Life and death are not divided. The very instant that the old year died, the new year was born ; and soon the dawn came " blushing o'er the world," as if such a thing as death were unknown. The bugles sounded the morning call, as they had sounded for the night's repose. Scarcely had we caught the last echoes, that, growing fainter and fainter, seemed to be wailing for the dying year, before a piercing blast announced his successor. The King is dead! Long live the King!

Moorish Castle.

CHAPTER II.

CLIMBING THE ROCK.

IT was a bright New-Year's morning, that first day of
1887, and how could we begin the year better than by
climbing to the top of the Rock to get the outlook over
land and sea? The ascent is not difficult, for though the
Rock is steep as well as high, a zigzag path winds up its
side, which to a good pedestrian is only a bracing walk,
while a lady can mount a little donkey and be carried to
the very top. If you have to go slowly, so much the better, for you will be glad to linger by the way. As you
mount higher and higher, the view spreads out wider and
wider. Below, the bay is placid as an inland lake, on
which ships of war are riding at anchor, "resting on their
shadows," while vessels that have brought supplies for the
garrison are unlading at the New Mole. Nor is the side
of the Rock itself wanting in beauty. Gibraltar is not a
barren cliff: its very crags are mantled with vegetation,
and wild flowers spring up almost as in Palestine. Those
who have made a study of its flora tell us that it has no
less than five hundred species of flowering plants and
ferns, of which but one-tenth have been brought from

abroad; all the rest are native. The sunshine of Africa rests in the clefts of the rocks; in every sheltered spot the vine and fig-tree flourish, and the almond-tree and the myrtle; you inhale the fragrance of the locust and the orange blossoms; while the clematis hangs out its white tassels, and the red geranium lights up the cold gray stone with rich masses of color.

Thus loitering by the way, you come at last to the top of the Rock, where a scene bursts upon you hardly to be found elsewhere in the world, since you are literally pinnacled in air, with a horizon that takes in two seas and two continents. You are standing on the very top of one of the Pillars of Hercules, the ancient Calpe, and in full view of the other, on the African coast, where, above the present town of Ceuta, whose white walls glisten in the sun, rises the ancient Abyla, the Mount of God. These are the two Pillars which to the ancient navigators set bounds to the habitable world.

On this point is the Signal Station, from which a constant watch is kept for ships entering the Straits. There was a tradition that it had been an ancient watch-tower of the Carthaginians, from which (as from Monte Pellegrino, that overlooks the harbor of Palermo) they had watched the Roman ships. But later historians think it played no great part in history or in war until the Rock served as a stepping-stone to the Moors in their invasion and conquest of Spain. When the Spaniards retook it, they gave this peak the name of "El Hacho," The Torch, because here beacon-fires were lighted to give warning in time of danger. A little house furnishes a shelter for the officer on duty, who from its flat roof, with his field-glass, sweeps the whole horizon, north and south, from the Sierra Nevada in Spain, to the long chain of the Atlas Mountains in Africa. Looking down, the Mediterranean is at your feet. There go the ships, with boats from either shore which dip their long lateen-sails as sea-gulls dip their wings, and sometimes fly over the waves as a bird flies through the air, even while large ships labor against the wind. As the current from the Atlantic flows steadily into the Mediterranean, if perchance the wind should blow from the same quarter, it is not an easy matter to get out of the Straits. Ships that have made the whole course of the Mediterranean are baffled here in the throat of the sea. Before the days of steam, mariners were subject to delays of weeks, an experience which was more picturesque than pleasant. Thirty years ago a friend of mine made a voyage from Boston to Smyrna in the Henry Hill, a ship which often took out missionaries to the East, and now had on board a mixed cargo of missionaries and rum! Whether it was a punishment for the latter, on her return she had head winds all the way; but in spite of them was able to make a slow progress by tacking from shore to shore, for which, however, she had less room as she came into the Straits, through which, as through a funnel, both wind and current set at times with such force as in this case detained the Bostonian *five weeks!* "The captain,"

THE SIGNAL STATION.

says my informant, " was a pretty good-natured man, but as he was a joint-owner of the ship, this long detention was very trying. But to me "—it is a lady who writes— " it was quite the reverse. I found it delightful to tack over to the side of Gibraltar every morning, and drift back every evening to the shores of Africa, with the little excitement from the risk of being boarded by pirates in the night ! I never tired of the brilliant sunsets, the gorgeous clouds, with the snow-capped mountains of Granada for a background. But for the captain (even with missionaries on board, who were returning to America) the head winds were too much for his temper, and after vainly striving day after day to get through the Straits, he would take off his cap, scratch his head, and shake his fists at the clouds !

" After tacking for three weeks off Gibraltar, wearing out our cordage and exhausting our larder, we put into the bay and anchored. Here we were surrounded by vessels from all parts of the world, and were so near the town that we could almost exchange greetings with those on shore. One Sunday the Spaniards had a bull-fight just across the Neutral Ground ; but I preferred a quiet New England Sabbath on shipboard.

" After lying at anchor in the bay for two weeks I went on shore one day to lunch with an American lady. Returning to the ship in the evening, I betook myself to my berth. At midnight I heard unusual sounds, clanking of chains, and sailors singing ' Heave ho !' From my porthole I could see an unusual stir, and dressing in haste went on deck. Sure enough the wind had changed, and all the vessels in the bay were alive with excitement. The captain was radiant. I could see his beaming face, for it was clear and beautiful as moonlight could make it. He invited me to stay on deck, sent for a cup of coffee, and made himself very agreeable. We were soon under way. I was in a kind of ecstasy with the novelty and the beauty of it all. The full moon, the grand scenery, the Pillars of Hercules, solemn in the moonlight, and the added charm of six hundred vessels, from large to small craft, all in full sail, made a rare picture. I sat on deck till morning, and certainly never saw a more beautiful sight than that fleet spreading its wings like a flock of mighty sea-birds, and moving off together from the Mediterranean into the Atlantic."

Such picturesque scenes are not so likely to be witnessed now; for since the introduction of steam the plain and prosaic, but very useful, "tug" tows off the windbound bark through the dreaded Straits into the open sea, where she can spread her wings and fly across the wide expanse of the ocean.

To-day, as we look down from the signal station, we see no gathered ships below waiting for a favoring breeze; the wind scarcely ripples the sea, and the boats glide gently whither they will, while here and there a great steamer from England, bound for Naples, or Malta, or India, appears on the horizon, marking its course by the long line of smoke trailing behind it.

To this wonderful combination of land and sea nothing can be added except by the changing light which falls upon it. For the fullest effect you must wait till sunset, when the evening gun has been fired, to signal the departing day, and its heavy boom is dying away in the distance,

"Swinging low with sullen roar."

Then the sky is aflame where the sun has gone down in the Atlantic; and as the last light from the west streams through the Straits, they shine as if they were the very gates of gold that open into a fairer world than ours.

2

CHAPTER III.

THE FORTIFICATIONS.

IF Gibraltar were merely a rock in the ocean, like the Peak of Teneriffe, its solitary grandeur would excite a feeling of awe, and voyagers up and down the Mediterranean would turn to this Pillar of Hercules as the great feature of the Spanish coast, a " Pillar " poised between sea and sky, with its head in the clouds and its base deep in the mighty waters. But Gibraltar is at the same time the strongest fortress in the world, and the interest of every visitor is to see its defences, in which the natural strength of the position has been multiplied by all the resources of modern warfare.

A glance at the map will show what is to be defended. The Rock is nearly three miles long, with a breadth of half to three quarters of a mile, so that the whole circuit is about seven miles. But not all this requires to be defended, for on the eastern side the cliff is so tremendous that there is no possibility of scaling it. It is fearful to stand on the brow and look down to where the waves are dashing more than a thousand feet below. The only approach must be by land from the

THE NEW MOLE AND ROSIA BAY.

north, or from the sea on the western side. As the latter lies along the bay, and is at the lowest level, it is the most exposed to attack. Here lies the town, which could easily be approached by an enemy if it were not for its artificial defences. These consist mainly of what is called the Line-Wall, a tremendous mass of masonry two miles long, relieved here and there by projecting bastions, with guns turned right and left, so as to sweep the face of the wall, if an enemy were to attempt to carry it by storm. Indeed the line defended is more than two miles long, if we follow it in its ins and outs; where the New Mole reaches out its long arm into the bay, with a line of guns on either side; followed by a re-entering curve round Rosia Bay, the little basin whose waters are so deep and still, that it is a quiet haven for unlading ships, but where an enemy would find himself in the centre of a circle of fire under which nothing could live; and if we include the batteries still farther southward, that are carried beyond Europa Point, until the last gun is planted under the eastern cliff, which is itself a defence of nature that needs no help from man.

Within the Line-Wall, immediately fronting the bay, are the casemates and barracks for the artillery regiments that are to serve the guns. The casemates are designed to be absolutely bomb-proof, the walls being of such thickness as to resist the impact of shot weighing hundreds of pounds, while the enormous arches overhead are made to withstand the weight and the explosion of

the heaviest shells. Such at least was the design of the
military engineers who constructed them: though, with
the new inventions in war, the monster guns and the new
explosives, it is hard to put any limit to man's power of
destruction. This Line-Wall is armed with guns of the
largest calibre, some of which are mounted on the parapet above, but the greater part are in the casemates below, and therefore nearer the level of the sea, so that
they can be fired but a few feet above the water, and
thus strike ships in the most vital part.

The latest pets of Gibraltar are a pair of twins—two
guns. each of which weighs a hundred tons! These are
guarded with great care from the too close inspection of
strangers. No description can give a clear impression of
their enormous size. In the early history of artillery, the
Turks cast some of the largest pieces in the world. Those
who have visited the East, may remember the huge can-
non-balls of stone, that may still be seen lying under the
walls of the Round Towers on the Bosphorus. But those
were pebbles compared with shot that can only be lifted
to the mouth of the guns by machinery. The bore of
these monsters would delight the soul of the Grand Turk,
for, (as a man could easily crawl into one of them,) if the
barbarous punishment of the old days were still reserved
for great offenders, a Pasha who had displeased the Sultan might easily be put in along with the cartridge, and
be rammed down and fired off!

The guns had recently been tried, and found to be per-

Painted by .... R.A.   Engraved by J Cochran.

GEORGE AUGUSTUS ELIOTT, LORD HEATHFIELD, BARON GIBRALTAR.

[The above portrait of "Old Eliott" was taken on his return from Gibraltar, in 1787, when he was the hero of England. The figure is drawn against a background of the clouds of war, with the cannon pointing downward, as when fired from the top of the Rock; while he holds firmly in his hand the key of the fortress he has won. The face is open, frank, and bold, with eyes looking straight before him, as if he did not fear any enemy. Many have remarked a likeness to Wellington, with a more prominent nose, a feature which Napoleon always liked in one whom he chose for a post of peculiar difficulty and danger.]

fect, though the explosion was not so terrible as had at
first been feared. There had been some apprehension
that a weapon which was to be so destructive to enemies, might not be an innocent toy to those who fired it;
that it might split the ear-drums of the gunners themselves. Some years ago I was at Syra, in the Greek Archi-
pelago, when the English ironclad Devastation was lying
in port, which had four thirty-five-ton guns, (the monsters of that day,) and one of her officers said that they
"never fired them except at sea, for that the discharge
in the harbor would break every window in the town."
But here the effect seems not to have been so great.
One who was present at the firing of one of the hundred-
ton guns, told me that all who stood round expected to be
deafened by the concussion. Yet when it came, they
turned and looked at each other with a mixture of surprise and disappointment. The sound was not in propor-
tion to the size. Indeed our Consul tells me that some of
the sixty-eight pounders are as ear-splitting as the hundred-ton guns. But an English gentleman whom I met
at Naples gave me a different report of his experience.
He had just come from Malta, where they have a
hundred-ton gun mounted on the ramparts. One day,
while at dinner in the hotel, they heard a crash, at
which all started from their seats, and rushed to the windows to throw them open, lest a second discharge should
leave not a pane of glass unbroken. But this came only
as they left the harbor. When about three miles at sea,

they saw the flash, which was followed by a boom such as they never heard before. It was the most awful thunder rolling over the deep in billows, like waves of the sea, filling the whole horizon with the vast, tremendous sound. It was as " the voice of God upon the waters."

But, of course, with the hundred-ton guns, as with any other, the main question is, not how much noise they make, but what is their power of destruction. Here the experiment was entirely satisfactory. It proved that a hundred-ton gun would throw a ball weighing 2,000 pounds over eight miles!* With such a range it would reach every part of the bay, and a brace of them, with the hundreds of heavy guns along the Line-Wall, might be relied upon to clear the bay of a hostile fleet, so that Gibraltar could hardly be approached by sea.

But these are not the whole of its defences; they are only the beginning. There are batteries in the rear of the town, as well as in front, that can be fired over the tops of the houses, so that, if an enemy were to effect a landing he would have to fight his way at every step. As you climb the Rock, it fairly bristles with guns. You cannot turn to the right or the left without seeing these open-mouthed monsters, and looking into their murder-

---

* The exact figures of this Armstrong Gun are: Weight, 101.2 tons. Length, 32.65 feet. Length of bore, 30.25 feet. Diameter of bore, 17.72 inches. Length of charge of powder, 5 feet. Weight of charge, 450 pounds. Weight of shot, 2,000 pounds. Velocity at the muzzle, 1,548 feet per second. At such velocity, a ball of such weight would have a "smashing effect" of 33,230 "foot-tons," and would penetrate 24.9 inches of wrought iron. Range, when fired at the highest elevation, over 8 miles.

ous throats. Everywhere it is nothing but guns, guns, guns! There are guns over your head and under your feet—

> "Cannon to the right of you,
> Cannon to the left of you;"

and what is still more, cannon pointed directly at you, till you almost feel as if they were aimed with a purpose, and as if they might suddenly open their mouths, and belch you forth, as the whale did Jonah, though not upon the land, but into the midst of the sea!

But my story is not ended. It is a good rule in description to keep the best to the last. The unique feature of Gibraltar—that in which it surpasses all the other fortresses of Europe, or of the world—is the Rock Galleries, to which I will now lead the way. These were begun more than a hundred years ago, during the Great Siege, which lasted nearly four years, when the inhabitants had no rest day nor night. For, though the French and Spanish besiegers had not rifled guns, nor any of the improved artillery of modern times, yet even with their smooth-bore cannon and mortars they managed to reach every part of the Rock. Bombs and shells were always flying over the town, now bursting in the air, and now falling with terrible destruction. So high did these missiles reach, that even the Rock Gun, on the very pinnacle of Gibraltar, was twice dismounted. Thus pursued to the very eagle's nest of their citadel, and finding no rest above ground, the besieged felt that their only shelter must be in the bowels of the earth, and gangs of convicts were set to work to blast out these long galleries, which we are now to visit.

As it is a two miles' walk through them, we may save our steps by riding as far as the entrance. It is an easy drive up to the Moorish Castle, built by the African invader who crossed the Straits in 711, and finding the south of Spain an easy conquest, resolved to establish himself in the country, and a few years later built this castle on a shoulder of the hill, where it has stood, frowning over land and sea for nearly twelve centuries.

Here we present an order from the Military Secretary, and the officer in charge details a gunner to conduct us through the galleries. The gate is opened, and we plunge in at once, beginning on the lower level. The excavation is just like that of a railway tunnel, except that no arches are required, as it is for the whole distance hewn through the solid rock, which is self-supporting.

But it is not a gloomy cavern that we are to explore, through which we can make our way only by the light of torches, for at every dozen yards there is a large port-hole, by which light is admitted from without, at all of which heavy guns are mounted on carriages, by which they can be swung round to any quarter.

After we have passed through one tier, perhaps a mile in length, we mount to a second, which rises above the other like the upper deck of an enormous line-of-battle ship. Enormous indeed it must be, if we can imagine a double-decker a mile long!

Following the galleries to the very end, we find them enlarged to an open space, called the Hall of St. George, in which Nelson was once fêted by the officers of the garrison. It must have been a proud moment when the defenders of the Great Fortress paid homage to the Conqueror of the sea. As they drank to the health of the hero of the Battle of the Nile, they could hardly have dreamed that a greater victory was yet to come ; and still less, that it would be a victory followed by mourning, when all the flags in Gibraltar would be hung at half-mast, as the flagship of Nelson anchored in the bay, with only his body on board, one week after the battle of Trafalgar.

As we tramped past these endless rows of cannon, it occurred to me that their simultaneous discharge must be very trying to the nerves of the artilleryman (if he has any nerves), as the concussion against the walls of rock is much greater than if they were fired in the open air, and I asked my guide if he did not dread it ? He confessed that he did; but added, like the plucky soldier that he was : " We've got to stand up to it !"

These galleries are all on the northern side of the Rock, which, as it is very precipitous, hardly needs such a defence. But it is the side which looks toward Spain, and is intended to command any advance against the fortress from the land. Keeping in mind the general shape

of the Rock as that of a lion, this is the Lion's head, and
as I looked up at it afterward from the Neutral Ground,
I could but imagine these open port-holes, with the sav-
age-looking guns peering out of them, to be the lion's teeth,
and thought what terror would be thrown into a camp of
besiegers if the monster should once open those ponderous
jaws and shake the hills with his tremendous roar.

It is not often that this roar is heard; but there is one
day in the year when it culminates, when the British
Lion roars the loudest. It is the Queen's birthday, when
the Rock Gun, mounted on the highest point of the
Rock, 1,400 feet in air, gives the signal; which is immediately caught up by the galleries below, one after the
other; and the batteries along the sea answer to those
from the mountain side, until the mighty reverberations
not only sweep round the bay, but across the Mediterranean, and far along the African shores. Nothing like
this is seen or heard in any other part of the world. The
only parallel to it is in the magnificent phenomena of
nature, as in a storm in the Alps, when

> "Not from one lone cloud,
> But every mountain now hath found a tongue,
> And Jura answers from her misty shroud
> Back to the joyous Alps that call to her aloud."

This is magnificent: and yet I trust my military friends
will not despise my sober tastes if I confess that this
" roar," if kept up for any length of time, would greatly
disturb the meditations of a quiet traveller like myself.

THE SALUTING BATTERY.

Indeed it would be a serious objection to living in Gibraltar that I should be compelled to endure the cannonading, which, at certain times of the year, makes the rocks echo with a deafening sound. I hate noise, and especially the noise of sharp explosions. I have always been of Falstaff's opinion, that

"But for those vile guns I would be a soldier."

But here the "vile guns" are everywhere, and though they may be quiet for a time, it is only to break out afterward and make themselves heard in a way that cannot but be understood.

As I have happened on an interval of rest, I have been surprised at the quietness of Gibraltar. In all the time of my stay I have not heard a single gun, except at sunrise and sunset, and at half-past nine o'clock for the soldiers to return to their barracks. There has not been even a salute, for, although there is on the Alameda a saluting battery, composed of Russian guns taken in the Crimean War, yet it is less often used than might be supposed, for the ships of war that come here are for the most part English (the French and Spaniards would hardly find the associations agreeable), and these are not saluted since they are *at home*, as much as if they were entering Portsmouth.

For these reasons I have found Gibraltar so quiet that I was beginning to think it a dull old Spanish town, fit for a retreat, if not for monks, at least for travellers and scholars, when the Colonial Secretary dispelled the illusion by saying, "Yes, it is very quiet just now; but wait a few weeks and you will have enough of it." As the spring comes on, the artillerymen begin their practice. The guns in the galleries are not used, but all the batteries along the sea, and at different points on the side of the Rock, some of which are mounted with the heaviest modern artillery, are let loose upon the town.

But this is not done without due notice. The order is published in the *Chronicle*, a little sheet which appears every morning, and lest it might not reach the eyes of all, messengers are sent to every house to give due warning, so that nervous people can get out of the way; but the inhabitants generally, being used to it, take no other precaution than to open their windows, which might otherwise be broken by the violence of the concussion. Lord Gifford, soldier as he is, said, "It is awful," pointing to the ceiling over his head, which had been cracked in many places so as to be in danger of falling, by the tremendous jar. He told me how one house had been so knocked to pieces that a piece of timber had fallen, nearly killing an officer. This is an enlivening experience, of which I should be sorry to deprive those who like it. But as some of us prefer to live in " the still air of delightful studies," I must say that I enjoy these explosions best at a distance, as even in an Alpine storm I would not have the lightning flashing in my very eyes, but rather lighting up the whole blackened sky, and the mighty thunder rolling afar off in the mountains.

CHAPTER IV.

ACCUSTOMED as we are to think of Gibraltar as a Fortress, we may forget that it is anything else. But it is an old Spanish town, quaint and picturesque as Spanish towns are apt to be, with twenty thousand inhabitants, in which the Spanish element, though subject to another and more powerful element, gives a distinct flavor to the place. Indeed, the mingling of the Spanish with the English, or the appearance of the two side by side, without mingling, furnishes a lively contrast, which is one of the most piquant features of this very miscellaneous and picturesque population.

Of course, in a garrison town the military element is first and foremost. As there are always five or six thousand troops in Gibraltar, it is perhaps the largest garrison in the British dominions, unless the troops in and around London be reckoned as a garrison. But that is rather an army, of which only a small part is in London itself, where a few picked regiments are kept as Household Troops, not only to insure the personal safety of the sovereign, but to keep up the state and dignity of the court; while other regiments are distributed in barracks within easy call in case of need, not for defence against foreign enemies so much as to preserve internal order ; to put down riot and insurrection; and thus guard what is not only the capital of Great Britain, but the commercial centre of the world.

Very different from this is a garrison town, where a large body of troops is shut up within the walls of a fortress. Here the military element is so absorbing and controlling, that it dominates the whole life of the place. Everything goes by military rule; even the hours of the day are announced by "gun-fire ;" the morning gun gives the exact minute at which the soldiers are to turn out of their beds, and the last evening gun the minute at which they are to "turn in," signals which, though for the soldiers only, the working population of the town find it convenient to adopt; and which outsiders *must* regard, since at these hours the gates are opened and shut; so that a large part of the non-military part of the population have to "keep step," almost as much as if they were marching in the ranks, since their rising up and their lying down, their goings out and their comings in, are all regulated by the fire of the gun or the blast of the bugle.

The presence of so large a body of troops in Gibraltar gives a constant animation to its streets, which are alive with red-coats and blue-coats, the latter being the uniform of the artillery. This is a great entertainment to an

American, to whom such sights in his own country are
rare and strange. A few years ago we had enough of
them when we had a million of men in arms, and the
land was filled with the sound of war. But since the
blessed days of peace have come we seldom see a soldier,
so that the parades in foreign capitals have all the charm
of novelty. In fondness for these I am as much "a boy"
as the youngest of my countrymen. Almost every hour
a company passes up the street, and never do I hear the
"tramp, tramp," keeping time to the fife and drum, that
I do not rush to the balcony to see the sight, and hear the
sounds which stir even my peaceful breast.

There is nothing that stirs me quite so much as the
bugle. Twice a day it startles us with its piercing blast,
as it follows instantly the gun-fire at sunrise and sunset.
But this does not thrill me as when I hear it blown on
some far-off height, and dying away in a valley below, or
answered back from a yet more distant point, like a
mountain echo. One morning I was taking a walk to
Europa Point, and as the path leads upward I came upon
several squads of buglers (I counted a dozen men in one of
them) practising their "calls." They were stationed at
different points on the side of the Rock, so that when one
company had given the signal, it was repeated by another
from a distance, bugle answering to bugle, precisely like
the echoes in the Alps, to which every traveller stops to
listen. So here I stopped to listen till the last note had
died away in the murmuring sea ; and then, as I went on

over the hill, kept repeating, as if it were a spell to call them back again:

> " Blow, bugles, blow,
> Set the wild echoes flying ! "

As the English are masters of Gibraltar, I am glad to see that they bring their English ideas and English customs with them. Nothing shows the thoroughly English character of the place more than the perfect quiet of the day of rest. Religious worship seems to be a part of the military discipline. On Sunday morning I heard the familiar sound of music, followed by the soldiers' tramp, and stepping to the balcony again, found a regiment on the march, not to parade but *to church*. Gibraltar has the honor of being the seat of an English bishop, because of which its modest church bears the stately name of a Cathedral; and here may be seen on a Sunday morning nearly all the officials of the place, from the Governor down; with the officers of the garrison: and probably the soldiers generally follow the example of their officers in attending the service of the Church of England. But they are not compelled to this against their own preferences. The Irish can go to mass, and the Scotch to their simpler worship. In all the churches there is a large display of uniforms, nor could the preachers address more orderly or more attentive listeners. The pastor of the Scotch church tells me that he is made happy when a Scotch regiment is ordered to Gibraltar, for then he is sure of a large array of stalwart Cameronians, among whom are always some who have the "gift of prayer," and know how to sing the "Psaumes of Dawvid." These brave Scots go through with their religious exercises almost with the stride of grenadiers, for they are in dead earnest in whatever they undertake, whether it be praying or fighting; and these are the men on whom a great commander would rely to lead a forlorn hope into the deadly breach; or, as an English writer has said, "to march first and foremost if a city is to be taken by storm!"

Besides the garrison, and the English or Spanish residents of Gibraltar, the town has a floating population as motley in race and color as can be found in any city on the Mediterranean. Indeed it is one of the most cosmopolitan places in the world. It is a great resort of political refugees, who seek protection under the English flag. As it is so close to Spain, it is the first refuge of Spanish conspirators, who, failing in their attempts at revolution, flee across the lines. Misery makes strange bedfellows. It must be strange indeed for those to meet here who in their own land have conspired with, or it may be against, each other.

Apart from these, there is a singular mixture of characters and countries, of races and religions. Here Spaniards and Moors, who fought for Gibraltar a thousand years ago, are at peace and good friends, at least so far as to be willing to cheat each other as readily as if they were of the same religion. Here are long-bearded Jews

3

in their gabardines; and Turks with their baggy trousers,
taking up more space than is allowed to Christian legs;
with a mongrel race from the Eastern part of the Mediterranean, known as Levantines; and another like unto
them, the Maltese; and a choice variety of natives of
Gibraltar, called " Rock scorpions," with Africans blacker
than Moors, who have perhaps crossed the desert, and
hail from Timbuctoo.   All these make a Babel of races
and languages, as they jostle each other in these narrow
and crowded streets, and bargain with each other, and, I
am afraid, sometimes swear at each other, in all the languages of the East.

Here is a field for the young American artists, who
after making their sketches in Florence and Rome and
Naples, sometimes come to Spain, but seldom take the
trouble to come as far as the Pillars of Hercules.   As an
old traveller, let me assure them that an artist in search
of the picturesque, or of what is curious in the study
of strange peoples, may find in Gibraltar, with its neighbor Tangier, (but three hours' sail across the Straits) subjects for his pencil as rich in feature, in color, and in cos-
tume, as he can find in the bazaars of Cairo or Constantinople.

CHAPTER V.

THE garrison of Gibraltar, in time of peace, numbers
five or six thousand men, made up chiefly of regiments brought home from foreign service, that are stationed here for a few months, or it may be a year or two,
not merely to perform garrison duty, but as a place of
rest to recover strength for fresh campaigns, from which
they can be ordered to any part of the Mediterranean or
to India. While here they are kept under constant
drill, yet not in such bodies as to make a grand military display, for there is no parade ground large enough
for the purpose. Gibraltar has no Champ de Mars on
which all the regiments can be brought into the field,
and go through with the evolutions of an army. If
the whole garrison is to be put under arms, it must be
marched out of the gates to the North Front, adjoining
the Neutral Ground, that it may have room for its military manœuvres. When our countryman General Craw-
ford, who commanded the Pennsylvania Reserves at the
Battle of Gettysburg, was here a few years since, the Gov-

ernor, Sir Fenwick Williams, gave him a review of four thousand men. But that was a mark of respect to a distinguished military visitor, and presented a sight rarely witnessed by the ordinary traveller. It was therefore a piece of good fortune to have an opportunity to see, though on a smaller scale, the splendid bearing of the trained soldiers of the British Army. One morning our Consul (always thoughtful of what might contribute to my pleasure) sent me word that there was to be a parade of one of the regiments of the garrison for the purpose of receiving new colors from the hands of the Governor. Hastening to the Alameda, (which is the only open space within the walls at once large enough and level enough even for a single regiment,) I found it already in position, the long scarlet lines forming three sides of a hollow square. Joining a group of spectators on the side that was open, we waited the arrival of the Governor, an interval well employed in some inquiries as to the corps that was to receive the honors of the day.

"What did you tell me was the name of this Regiment?" "The South Staffordshire!" But that is merely the name of a county in England, which conveys no meaning to an American. And yet the name caught my ear as one that I had heard before. "Was not this one of the Regiments that served lately in the Soudan?" It was indeed the same, and I at once knew more of it than I had supposed. As I had been twice in Egypt, I was greatly interested in the expedition up the Nile for the relief of Khartoum and the rescue of General Gordon, and had followed its progress in the English papers, where, along with the Black Watch and other famous troops, I had seen frequent mention of the South Staffordshire Regiment. As the expedition was for months the leading feature of the London illustrated papers, they were filled with pictures of the troops, engaged in every kind of service, sometimes looking more like sailors than soldiers, from which, however, they were ready, at the first alarm, to fall into ranks and march to battle. Many of the comrades who sailed from England with them left their bones on the banks of the Nile.

With this recent history in mind, I could not look in the faces of the brave men who had made all these marches, and endured these fatigues, and fought these battles, without my heart beating fast. It beat faster still when I learned that the campaign in Egypt was only the last of a long series of campaigns, reaching over not only many years, but almost two centuries! The history of this regiment is worth the telling, if it were only to show of what stuff the British Army is made, and how the traditions of a particular corps, passing down from sire to son, remain its perpetual glory and inspiration.

The South Staffordshire Regiment is one of the oldest in the English Army, having been organized in the reign of Queen Anne, when the great Marlborough led her troops to foreign wars. But it does not appear to have fought under Marlborough, having been early transferred

to the Western Hemisphere. After four years' service
at home it was sent to the West Indies, where it remained nearly *sixty years*, its losses by death being made
good by fresh recruits from England, so that its organiza-
tion was kept intact. Returning home in 1765, it was
stationed in Ireland till the cloud began to darken over
the American Colonies, when it was one of the first corps
despatched across the Atlantic. As an American, I could
not but feel the respect due to a brave enemy on learning
that this very regiment that I saw before me *had fought
at Bunker Hill!* From Boston it was ordered to New
York, where it remained till the close of the war. No
doubt it often paraded on the Battery, as to-day it parades on the Alameda. After the war it was stationed
several years in Nova Scotia.

From that time it has had a full century of glory, serving now in the West Indies, and now at the Cape of Good
Hope, and then coming back across the Atlantic to the
River Plate in South America, where it distinguished itself at the storming and capture of Monte Video, and afterward fought at Buenos Ayres. But the "storm centre" in the opening nineteenth century was to be, not
in America, North or South, nor in Africa, but in
Europe, in the wars of Napoleon. This regiment was
with Sir John Moore when he fell at Corunna, and afterward followed the Iron Duke through Spain, fighting in
the great battle of Salamanca, and later with Sir Thomas
Graham at Vittoria, and in the siege and storming of San

Sebastian. It was part of the army that crossed the Bidassoa, and made the campaign of 1813–14 in the South of France. After the fall of Napoleon it returned home, but on his return from Elba was immediately ordered back to the Continent, and arrived at Ostend, too late to take part in the Battle of Waterloo, but joined the army and marched with it to Paris.

When the great disturber of the peace of the Continent was sent to St. Helena, Europe had a long rest from war; but there was trouble in other parts of the world, and in 1819 the regiment was again at the Cape of Good Hope, fighting the Kaffirs; from which it went to India, and thence to Burmah, where it served in the war of 1824–26. This is the war which has been made familiar to American readers in the Life of the Missionary Judson, who was thrown into prison at Ava, (as the King made no distinction between Englishmen and Americans), confined in a dungeon, and chained to the vilest malefactors, in constant danger of death, till the advance of the British army up the Irrawaddi threw the tyrant into a panic of terror, when he sent for his prisoner to go to the British camp and make terms with the conquerors. England made peace, but the regiment was half destroyed, having lost in Burmah eleven officers and five hundred men.

The ten years of peace that followed were spent in Bengal. When at last the regiment was called home, it was stationed for a few years in the Ionian Islands, in Jamaica, Honduras, and Nova Scotia. Then came the Russian War, when it was sent to Turkey, and fought at the Alma and Inkerman, and through the long siege of Sebastopol. Only a single year of peace followed, and it was again ordered to India, where the outbreak of the mutiny threatened the loss of the Indian Empire, and by forced marches reached Cawnpore in time to defeat the Sepoy army; from which it marched to Lucknow, where it was part of the fiery host that stormed the Kaiser-Bagh, where it suffered fearful loss, but the siege was raised and Lucknow delivered; after which, in a campaign in Oude, it helped to stamp out the mutiny.

Its last campaign was in Egypt, where it went up the Nile as a part of the River Column, hauling its boats over the cataracts, and was the first regiment that reached Korti. From this point it kept along the course of the river toward Berber (while another column, mounted on camels, made the march across the desert), and with the Black Watch bore the brunt of the fighting in the battle of Kirbekan, in which the commander of the column and the colonel of the regiment both fell.*

* A letter received from Sir Charles Wilson, who was in the column that crossed the desert, and who went up the Nile and arrived in sight of Khartoum only to learn that the city had fallen and Gordon been killed, speaks warmly of both these officers, his old companions in arms. He says : " General Earle, who was killed at Kirbekan, was a regimental officer in the Guards, and had been on the staff in Canada and India—in both cases, I think, as military secretary to the Viceroy. He was much beloved by every one. Colonel Earle, who commanded the South Staffordshire Regi-

Such is the story of a hundred and fifty years. Of the hundred and eighty-four years that the Regiment has been in existence, it has spent a hundred and thirty-four—all but fifty—in foreign service, in which it has fought in thirty-eight battles, and has left the bones of its dead in every quarter of the globe. Was there ever a Roman legion that could show a longer record of war and of glory?

And now this British legion, with a history antedating the possession of Gibraltar itself, (for it was organized in 1702, two years before the Rock was captured from Spain,) had been brought back to this historic ground, bringing with it its old battle-flags, that had floated on so many fields, which, worn by time and torn by shot and shell, it was now to surrender, to be taken back to England and hung in the oldest church in Staffordshire as the proud memorials of its glory, while it was to receive new colors, to be borne in future wars. The rents in its ranks had been filled by new recruits, so that it stood full a thousand strong, its burnished arms glistening as if those who bore them had never been in the heat of battle. In the hollow square in which it was drawn up were its mounted officers, waiting the arrival of the Governor, who presently rode upon the ground, with Major-General Walker, the Commander of the Infantry Brigade, at his

ment, was also killed at Kirbekan. He originally rose from the ranks, and was looked upon as one of the best regimental officers up the Nile.

side; followed by other officers, who took position in the
rear, according to their rank.   The band struck up "God
save the Queen," and the troops, wheeling into column,
began the "march past," moving with such firm and even
tread that it seemed as if the regiment had but one
body and one soul.   After a series of evolutions it was
again formed in a square, for a ceremony that was half
military and half religious, for in such pageants the
Church of England always lends its presence to the scene.
I had read of military mass in the Russian army, when
the troops drawn up in battle array, fall upon their knees,
while the Czar, prostrating himself, prays apparently
with the utmost devotion for the blessing of Almighty
God upon the Russian arms!   Something of the same effect was produced here, when the Bishop of Gibraltar in
his robes came forward with his assistant clergy.   At
once the band ceased; the troops stood silent and rever-
ent.   The silence was first broken by the singing of a
Hymn, whose rugged verse had a strange effect, as given
by the Regimental Choir.   I leave to my readers to imagine the power of these martial lines sung by those sten-
torian voices:

> When Israel's Chief in days of yore,
>   Thy banner, Lord, flung out,
> Old Kishon's tide ran red with gore,
>   Dire was the Pagan rout.
>
> And later, when the Roman's eye
>   Turned upward in despair,

The Cross, that flickered in the sky,
  Made answer to his prayer.

So, Lord, to us Thy suppliants now,
  Bend Thou a gracious ear,
And mark, and register the vow
  We make before Thee here.

Through fire and steel, 'mid weal or woe,
  Unwavering and in faith,
Where'er these sacred banners go,
  We'll follow, to the death.

We'll follow, strengthened by the might
  That comes of trust in Thee,
And if we conquer in the fight,
  Thine shall the glory be:

Or if Thy wisdom wing the ball,
  And life or limb be riven,
The Cross we gaze on as we fall
  Shall point the way to Heaven.

When this song of battle died away, the voice of the
Bishop was heard in a prayer prepared for the occasion.
Some may criticise it as implying that the God of
Battles must always be on the side of England. But
such is the character of all prayers offered in time of war.
Making this allowance, it seems as if the feeling of the
hour could not be more devoutly expressed than in the
following:

ALMIGHTY and most merciful Father, without whom nothing is
strong, nothing is holy, we come before Thee with a deep sense
of Thine exceeding Majesty and our own unworthiness, praying

Thee to shed upon us the light of Thy countenance, and to hallow and sanctify the work in which we are this day engaged.

We beseech Thee to forward with Thy blessing, the presentation to this Regiment of the Colors which are henceforth to be carried in its ranks; and with all lowliness and humility of spirit, we presume to consecrate the same in Thy great name, to the cause of peace and happiness, truth and justice, religion and piety. We humbly pray that the time may come when the sound of War shall cease to be heard in the world; but forasmuch as to our mortal vision that blessed consummation seems still far distant, we beseech Thee so to order the course of events that these colors shall be unfurled in the face of an enemy only for a righteous cause. And in that dark hour may stain and disgrace fall upon them never; but being borne aloft as emblems of loyalty and truth, may the brave who gather round them go forward conquering for the right, and maintaining, as becomes them, the honor of the British Crown, the purity of our most holy faith, the majesty of our laws, and the influence of our free and happy constitution. Finally, we pray that Thy servants here present, not forgetful of Thine exceeding mercies vouchsafed to their regiment in times gone by, and that all the forces of our Sovereign Lady the Queen, wherever stationed and however employed, may labor through Thy grace to maintain a conscience void of offence towards Thee and towards man, always remembering that of soldier and of civilian the same account shall be taken, and that he is best prepared to do his duty, and to meet death, let it come in what form it may, who in the integrity of a pure heart is able to look to Thee as a God reconciled to him through the blood of the Atonement. Grant this, O Lord, for Thine only Son Jesus Christ's sake! Amen.

Then followed the usual prayer for the Queen:

O Lord, our Heavenly Father, high and mighty, King of kings, Lord of lords, the only Ruler of princes, who dost from Thy throne behold all the dwellers upon earth, most heartily we beseech Thee with Thy favor to behold our most gracious Sovereign Lady Queen Victoria, and so replenish her with the grace of Thy Holy Spirit that she may always incline to Thy will and walk in Thy way; en-

due her plenteously with heavenly gifts; grant her in health and
wealth long to live; strengthen her that she may vanquish and
overcome all her enemies; and finally, after this life, she may at-
tain everlasting joy and felicity, through Jesus Christ our Lord!
Amen.

The grace of our Lord Jesus Christ, and the love of God, and
the fellowship of the Holy Ghost, be with us all evermore! Amen.

The service ended, the Governor, dismounting from
his horse, took the place of the Bishop in a service which
had a sacred as well as patriotic character. Two officers, the youngest of the Regiment, advancing, surrendered the old flags, which had been carried for so many
years and through so many wars, and then each bend-
ing on one knee, received from his hands the new colors
which were to have a like glorious history. As they rose
from their knees, the Governor remounted his horse,
and from the saddle delivered an address as full of
patriotic sentiment, of loyalty to the Queen and country,
and as spirit-stirring to the brave men before him, as if
they were to be summoned to immediate battle. With
that he turned and galloped off the ground, while the
Regiment unfurling its new standards, with drums beating and band playing, marched proudly away.

As it wound up the height, the long scarlet line had a
most picturesque effect. It has been objected to these
brilliant uniforms that they make the soldiers too conspicuous a mark for the sharpshooters of the enemy. But,
however it may be in war, nothing can be finer on pa-

rade. Our modern architects and decorators, who attach
so much importance to color, and insist that everything,
from cottage to castle, should be "picked out in red,"
would have been in ecstasies at the colors which that day
gleamed among the rocks and trees of Gibraltar.

Indeed, if you should happen to be sauntering on the
Alameda just at evening, as the sunset-gun is fired, and
should look upward to see the smoke curling away, you
might see above it a gathering of black clouds—the sure
sign of the coming of the terrible East wind known as
the "Levanter"; and if at the same moment the after-
glow of the dying day should touch a group of soldiers
standing on the mountain's crest (where colors could be
clearly distinguished even if figures were confused), it
might seem as if that last gleam under the shadow of the
clouds were itself the red cross of England soaring against
a dark and stormy sky.

This was the brilliant side of war: pity that there
should be another side! But the next day, walking near
the barracks, I met a company with reversed arms bearing the body of a comrade to the grave. There was no
funeral pomp, no waving plumes nor roll of muffled
drums: for it was only a common soldier, who might
have fallen on any field, and be buried where he fell, with
not a stone to mark his resting-place. But for all that, he
may have been a true hero; for it is such as he, the unknown brave, who have fought all the battles and gained
all the victories of the world.

Turning from this scene, I thought how hard was the fate of the English soldier : to be an exile from the land of his birth, " a man without a country " ; who may be ordered to any part of the world (for such is the stern necessity, if men are to defend " an Empire on which the sun never sets") ; serving in many lands, yet with a home in none ; to sleep at last in a nameless grave ! Such has been the fate of many of that gallant regiment which I saw marching so proudly yesterday. Their next campaign may be in Central Asia, fighting the Russians in Afghanistan, amid the snows of the Himalayas. If so, I fear it may be said of them with sad, prophetic truth, as they go into battle :

> " Ah ! few shall part where many meet ;
> The snow shall be their winding-sheet ;
> And every turf beneath their feet
> Shall be a soldier's sepulchre."

CHAPTER VI.

SOCIETY IN GIBRALTAR.

THE best thing that I find in any place is the men that are in it. Strong walls and high towers are grand, but after a while they oppress me by their very massiveness, unless animated by a living presence. Even the great guns, those huge monsters that frown over the ramparts, would lose their majesty and terror, if there were not brave men behind them. And so, after I had surveyed Gibraltar from every point of land and sea; after I had been round about it, and marked well its towers and its bulwarks; to complete the enjoyment I had but one wish—to sit down in some quiet nook and talk it all over.

There is no man in the world whom I respect more than an old soldier. He is the embodiment of courage and of all manly qualities, and he has given his life to his country. And if he bears in his person the scars of honorable wounds, I look up to him with a feeling of veneration. Of such characters no place has more than Gibraltar, which perhaps may be considered the centre of the military life of England. True, the movements of the Army are directed by orders from the Horse Guards in London.

But here the military feature is the predominant, if not the exclusive, one; while in London a few thousand troops would be lost in a city of five millions of inhabitants. Here the outward and visible sign is ever before you; regiments whose names are historical, are always coming and going; and if you are interested in the history of modern wars, (as who can fail to be, since it is a part of the history of our times?) you may not only read about them in the Garrison Library, but see the very men that have fought in them. Here is a column coming up the street! I look at its colors, and read the name of a regiment already familiar through the English papers; that has shown the national pluck and endurance in penetrating an African forest or an Indian jungle, or in climbing the Khyber Pass in the Himalayas to settle accounts with the Emir of Cabul. There must be strange meetings of old comrades here, as well as new companionships formed between those who have fought under the same royal standard, though in different parts of the world. A regiment recalled from Halifax is quartered near another just returned from Natal or the Cape of Good Hope; while troops from Hong Kong, or that have been up the Irrawaddi to take part in the late war in Upper Burmah, can exchange experiences with their brother soldiers from the other side of the globe. Almost all the regiments collected here have figured in distant campaigns, and the officers that ride at their head are the very ones that led them to victory. To a heart that is

4

not so dead but that it can still be stirred by deeds of
daring, there is nothing more thrilling than to sit under
the guns of the greatest fortress in the world, and listen
to the story as it comes from the lips of those who were
actors in the scenes.

But it would be a mistake to suppose that the society
of Gibraltar is confined to men. The home instincts are
strong in English breasts; and wherever they go they
carry their household gods with them. In my wanderings about the world, it has been my fortune to visit por-
tions of the British Empire ten thousand miles away
from the mother country; yet in every community there
was an English stamp, a family likeness to the old island
home. Hence it is that in the most remote colony there
are the elements of a good society. Whatever country
the English may enter, even if it be in the Antipodes, as
soon as they have taken root and become established they
send back to England for their wives and daughters, that
they may renew the happy life that they have lived before, so that the traveller who penetrates the interior of
Australia, of New Zealand, or Van Dieman's Land, is surprised to find, even "in the bush," the refinement of an
English home.

This instinct is not lost, even when they are in camps
or barracks. If you visit a "cantonment" in Upper India, you will find the officers with their families about
them. The brave-hearted English women "follow the
drum" to the ends of the earth; and I have sometimes

thought that their husbands and brothers owed part of their indomitable resolution to the inspiration of their wives and sisters.

It is this feature of garrison life, this union of "fair women and brave men," which gives such a charm to the society of Gibraltar—a union which is more complete here than in most garrison towns, because the troops stay longer, and there is more opportunity for that home-life which strangers would hardly believe to exist. Most travellers see nothing of it. Indeed it is probable that they hardly think of Gibraltar as having any home-life, since its population is always on the come and go; living here only as in a camp, and to-morrow

> " Folding its tents like the Arabs,
> And silently stealing away."

This is partly true. Soldiers of course are subject to orders, and the necessities of war may cause them to be embarked at an hour's notice. But in time of peace they may remain longer undisturbed. Regiments which have done hard service in India are sometimes left here to re-cruit even for years, which gives their officers opportunity to bring their families, whose presence makes Gibraltar seem like a part of England itself, as if it were no farther away than the Isle of Wight. This it is which makes life here quite other than being imprisoned in a fortress. I may perhaps give some glimpses of these interiors (without publicity to what is private and sacred), which I depict simply that I may do justice to a place to which I came as a stranger, and from which I depart as a friend.

Just before I left America, I was present at a breakfast given to M. de Lesseps on his visit to America to attend the inauguration of Bartholdi's Statue of Liberty. As I sat opposite the "grand Français," I turned the conversation to Spain, to which I was going, and where I knew that he had spent many years. He took up the subject with all his natural fire, and spoke of the country and the people in a way to add to my enthusiasm. Next to him sat Chief Justice Daly, who kindled at the mention of Spain, and almost "raved" (if a learned Judge ever "raves") about Spanish cathedrals. He had continued his journey to the Pillars of Hercules, and said that "in all his travels he had never spent a month with more pleasure than in Gibraltar." He had come with letters to the Governor, Lord Napier of Magdala, which at once opened all doors to him. Wishing to smooth my path in the same way, the English Minister at Madrid, who had shown me so much courtesy there, gave me a letter to the Colonial Secretary, Lord Gifford, who received me with the greatest kindness, and took me in at once to the Governor, who was equally cordial in his welcome.

The position of Governor of Gibraltar is one of such distinction as to be greatly coveted by officers in the English army. It is always bestowed on one of high rank, and generally on some old soldier who has distinguished

himself in the field. Among the late Governors was Sir
Fenwick Williams, who, with only a garrison of Turks,
under the command of four or five English officers, defended Kars, the capital of Armenia, in 1855, repelling an
assault by the Russians when they endeavored to take it
by storm, and yielding at last only to famine; and Lord
Napier of Magdala, who, born in Ceylon, spent the earlier
part of his military life in India, where he fought in the
Great Mutiny, and distinguished himself at Lucknow.
Ten years later he led an English army (though composed
largely of Indian troops, with the Oriental accompaniment
of guns and baggage-trains carried on the backs of camels
and elephants) into Abyssinia, and took the capital in an
assault in which King John was slain, and the missionaries and others, whom he had long held as prisoners and
captives, were rescued. He was afterward commander-
in-chief of the forces in India, and, when he retired from
that, no position was thought more worthy of his rank
and services than that of Governor of Gibraltar, a fit termination to his long and honored career.

The present Governor is a worthy successor to this
line of distinguished men. Sir Arthur Hardinge is
the son of Lord Hardinge, who commanded the army
in India a generation ago. Brought up as it were in a
camp, he was bred as a soldier, and when little more than
a boy accompanied his father to the wars, serving as aide-
de-camp through the Sutlej campaign in 1845–46, and
was in the thick of the fight in some hard-fought battles,

in one of which, at Ferozeshah, he had a horse shot under him. When the Crimean War broke out he was ordered to the field, and served in the campaign of 1854–55,
being at the Alma and at Inkerman, and remaining to the
close of the siege of Sebastopol. Here he had rapid promotion, besides receiving numerous decorations from the
Turkish Government, and being made Knight of the
Legion of Honor. Returning to England, he seems to
have been a favorite at court and at the Horse Guards,
being made Knight Commander of the Bath, honorary
Colonel of the King's Royal Rifle Corps, and Extra
Equerry to the Queen, his honors culminating in his present high position of Governor and Commander-in-chief of
Gibraltar.

The politeness of the Governor did not end with his
first welcome: it was followed by an invitation to his New
Year's Reception. It was but a few weeks since he had
taken office; and, wishing to do a courtesy to the citizens
of Gibraltar as well as to the officers of the garrison, both
were included in the invitation. The Government House
was the one place where all—soldiers and civilians—could
meet on common ground, and form the acquaintance, and
cultivate the friendly feeling, so important to the happiness of a community shut up within the limits of a fortress. Although I was a stranger, the Consul desired me
to attend, as it would give me the opportunity to see in
a familiar way the leading men of Gibraltar, civil and
military, and further, as, owing to the recent death of his

son, he could not be present nor any of his family, so that I should be the only representative of our country.

It was indeed a notable occasion. The Government House is an old Convent, which still retains its ancient and venerable look, though the flag floating over it, and the sentry marching up and down before the door, tell that it is now the seat of English power. To-night it took on its most festive appearance, entrance and stairway being hung with flags, embowered in palms, and wreathed with vines and ferns and flowers; and when the officers appeared in their uniforms, and the military band filled the place with stirring music, it was a brilliant scene.

The gathering was in a large hall, part of which was turned to a purpose which to some must have seemed strangely incongruous with the sacred associations of the place: for in the old Spanish days this was a Convent of the Franciscan Friars, who, if they ever revisit the place of their former habitation, must have been shocked to find their chapel turned into a place for music and dancing, and to hear the "sound of revelry by night," where they were wont to say midnight mass, and to offer prayers for the quick and dead!

While this was going on in one part of the hall, at the other end the Governor sat on a dais, quietly enjoying the meeting of old friends and the making of new ones. It was my good fortune to be one of the group, which gave me the best possible opportunity to see the society of Gibraltar: for here it was all gathered under

one roof. Of course it was chiefly military. There was a
brilliant array of officers—generals, colonels, and majors;
while in still larger number were captains and lieutenants, in their gay uniforms, who, if they did not exactly
realize my idea of

" Whiskered Pandours and fierce Hussars,"

looked like the brave and gallant Englishmen they were.
Nor were they alone: for there were civilians also—mag-
istrates and lawyers and judges; and, better still, the
lovely English women, who are the ornament of every
English colony. All received me with a manner so cordial as assured me that I was not to be treated with cold
formality as a stranger. If I had come into a camp of
American officers, I could not have had a more hearty
welcome.

At length the clock struck the hour of midnight, and I
rose to take leave of the Governor; but he answered,
"No, that will never do; you must take a lady out to
supper." Being under military orders, I could but obey,
and, essaying for the first time the part of a Spanish cav-
alier, conducted a Spanish lady into the dining-hall. This
is a historical apartment, in which have been fêted all the
royalties that have visited Gibraltar. On the walls are
hung the portraits of the Governors from the beginning
of the English occupation in 1704, among which every
visitor looks for that of "Old Eliott," the defender of
the place in the great siege. He was followed by a long

succession of brave men, who, in keeping Gibraltar, felt they were guarding the honor of England.

After this pleasant duty had been performed, I returned to the Governor to "report" that "I had obeyed his orders," and that "in taking leave, I could only express the wish that Gibraltar might never be attacked in any other way than it had been that evening," adding that "if he should treat all my countrymen as he had treated me, I could promise him on their part, as on mine, an unconditional surrender!"

Thus introduced, I found myself at home in a circle which included men who had seen service in all parts of the world. Next to the Governor I was attracted by a grand old officer whom I had observed on the parade, his breast being covered with decorations won in many wars. This was Major-General Walker, who has been in the army for a large part of the reign of Queen Victoria. As long ago as the Anglo-Russian war, he was an adjutant in one of the regiments sent to the Crimea, where he fought at the Alma and at Inkerman, and took part in the long siege of Sebastopol. Eager to be in the post of danger, he volunteered for a night attack, in which he led a party that took and destroyed a Russian rifle-pit. Soon after he was dangerously wounded in the trenches, and his right arm amputated, for which he was promoted and received a number of decorations. He afterward served throughout the campaign of 1860, in China.*

* War Services of General Officers, in Hart's Annual Army List for 1882.

Lord Gifford, though too young for service dating so far back, and of such slender figure that he looks more like a university student than like a soldier, was the hero of the Ashantee War, who led his men through forest and jungle, in the face of the savage foe, to the capture of Coomassie, for which he received the Victoria Cross, the proud distinction of a British soldier.

A little volume published in England, entitled "The Victoria Cross in the Colonies," by Lieutenant-Colonel Knollys, F.R.G.S., gives the following sketch of this gallant officer.

"The hero of the Ashantee War, 1873-74, was undoubtedly Ederic, third Baron Gifford. Born in 1849, he entered the Eighty-third Regiment as ensign in 1869, became lieutenant the following year, and in 1873 was transferred to the Twenty-fourth Regiment. He was one of the body of volunteers who accompanied Sir Garnet Wolseley to the Gold Coast. Appointed to train and command the Winnebeh company of Russell's native regiment, he took part in the defence of Absacampa and the defeat of the Ashantee army. He subsequently, for several weeks, performed the duties of adjutant to Russell's regiment. When the Ashantee territory was invaded, to Lord Gifford was assigned the command of a scouting party. This party was fifty strong, and composed of men from the West India Regiment of Houssas, Kossos, and Bonny natives.

"Early on the morning of January 6th, 1874, Gifford, with his scouts, crossed the Prah in canoes, and explored the country on both sides of the road to Coomassie. The rest of the army crossed by the bridge the same day. Marching some five miles ahead of the advance guard, he reached a village called Essiaman, and found that it was occupied by an Ashantee detachment, which, on advancing, he at once attacked and put to flight, losing only one man severely wounded. Advancing to a village called Akrofumin, he discovered that it was held by the Ashantees; but not being able to ascertain their strength, which he believed to be superior to his own, he prudently contented himself with observing them.

"After remaining in this critical position for several days, he had the satisfaction of seeing the enemy retire. He then pushed on—indeed never left off pushing on in the most daring yet skilful manner till Coomassie was reached—always keeping well ahead. His scouts were devoted to Lord Gifford, 'whose docile savages,' writes an historian of the campaign, 'worshipped the English gentleman for his superior skill and spirit in climbing that steep barrier range, the Adansi Hills, dividing the Assin from the Ashantee country. The night previous to the action at Amoaful, he carefully reconnoitred the enemy's position, and during the fight he was, with his gallant little band, as usual, well in advance.

"The next day he was sent to reconnoitre the village of Becqua. He had got close up when some twenty Ashantees sprang up in the bush and fired, but providentially without effect. On receipt of his report Sir Garnet Wolseley despatched a strong force to capture the place. Gifford's scouts led, followed by a body of Houssas, Russell's Regiment, and the Naval Brigade, the Forty-second Highlanders, and a company of the Twenty-third Royal Welsh Fusileers acting as supports. As soon as the firing began, Gifford, followed by his handful of scouts, rushed on, and dashed into the town, though it was occupied by a thousand Ashantees. The Houssas, for once, could not be induced to charge; they persisted in lying down and firing unaimed shots into the bush.

"In the meantime Lord Gifford and his party were exposed to the concentrated fire of the defenders. His best scout was killed, and he and all his men were wounded. In fact, he was in an almost desperate situation. On this he shouted to the Naval Brigade to come to his assistance. With a cheer the gallant fellows replied to the appeal, and at their charge the enemy fled.

"Three days later the action of Ordahsu took place, Coomassie was entered, and the campaign was virtually at an end.

"From that time Lord Gifford, there being no further need for his services as a scout, acted as aide-de-camp to Sir Garnet Wolseley. During the whole war this young, slight, modest-looking lad had displayed the greatest enterprise and intrepidity, and rendered the most valuable services. Fortune had in this case certainly favored the brave; for notwithstanding unremitting exertions and constant exposure both to climate and the bullets of the enemy, he escaped disease, and was only once wounded. Modest as he was brave, he never sought to make capital out of his exploits. They were, however, too conspicuous to escape notice, and he was repeatedly mentioned in despatches.

"On his return to England, he paid a visit to his regiment, the Twenty-fourth, then stationed at Aldershot. He was received with the greatest enthusiasm by both men and officers. The former carried him shoulder-high into camp, and the latter entertained him at dinner; yet he was as unaffected and simple as if he had only returned from an ordinary duty. For his daring conduct on the Gold Coast he was granted the Victoria Cross."

It was a privilege to spend an hour with General Walker at his own table, and to draw him into conversation on the wars in which he had taken part, and the great soldiers who had been his companions in arms. Of his own part in these events he spoke very modestly, like the true soldier that he is; though no modesty could hide the story told by that empty sleeve of the arm that he had left in the trenches at Sebastopol. From the Southeastern corner of Europe to the eastern coast of Asia, is a long stretch round the globe, but here, when the scene of war was transferred from Russia to China, we find the same gallant officer among the foremost in the storming of the Taku forts, and with the combined French and English army that fought its way to Peking.

As the house of the Major General stands on the Line-

Wall, it is close to the enormous batteries in the casemates below, (while one of the hundred-ton guns is
mounted near the Alameda, quite " within speaking distance,") and must be rudely rocked by the thunder which
shakes even the solid ground like an earthquake. " What
do you do at such a time?" I asked of the ladies of the
family, to which they answered gayly, " Oh, we don't
mind it." They took good care, however, to take down
their mirrors, and to lay away their glass and china, lest
they should be shattered in pieces. Then they threw
open their windows, and let the explosion come. For me
this would be a trifle too near, and with all my love for
Gibraltar, I do not think I should choose a hundred-ton
gun as a next-door neighbor.

As I rose to leave, I found horses saddled and bridled
at the door, on which the General and his niece were
about to take their afternoon ride, for the officers in Gibraltar are not so shut up within its walls, that they cannot
take their pleasure as if they were in the field. True, the
Rock does not offer a very wide space for excursions, but
the gay troopers of both sexes have but to ride out of the
Northern gate, and cross the Spanish lines, and the whole
country is before them. One day I met the Governor
coming in at full speed, with his staff behind him; and
almost daily there are riding parties or hunting parties,
which go off for hours, and come back with the ruddy
English glow of health upon their faces.

Indeed if one had to go about on foot, he need not feel

as if he were shut up in a fortress-prison, for there are
pleasant walks over the Rock, leading to many a nook,
from which one may look off upon the sea, where, if he
has an agreeable companion, the hours will not seem long.
If for a few months the climate has a little too much of
the warmth of Africa, there is a delightful promenade
along the Alameda, where friends may saunter on summer evenings, inhaling the fresh breezes; or sit under
the trees, and (as they listen to the bands playing the
familiar airs of England) talk of their dear native island.

WALK IN THE ALAMEDA GARDENS.

CHAPTER VII.

THE GREAT SIEGE.

ALTHOUGH Gibraltar is the greatest fortress in the world, if it were only that, it would not have half the interest which it now has. The supreme interest of the Rock is in the record of centuries that is graven on its rugged front. For nearly eight hundred years it was the prize of war between the Spaniard and the Moor, and its legends are all of battle and of blood. Ten times it was besieged and passed back and forth from conqueror to conqueror, the Cross replacing the Crescent, and the Crescent the Cross. Ten times was the battle lost and won. When, at last, in 1598 the Spaniards drove the Moors out of Spain, they remained masters of Gibraltar, and held it with undisputed sway for a little more than a hundred years. They might have held it still but for a surprise, hardly worthy to be called a siege; for the place was taken by a *coup de main*, that is one of the strangest incidents of history. It was the War of the Spanish Succession, waged by half Europe to determine which of two incompetents should occupy the throne of Spain. The English sent a squadron into the Mediterranean, under Sir

George Rooke. who, after cruising about and accomplish-
ing little, bethought himself, in order not to return in complete failure, to try his hand on Gibraltar. The place was
well fortified, with a hundred guns, but inside the walls
only a hundred and fifty men (a man and a half to a
gun!), so that it could offer but a brief resistance to a
bombardment, and thus the Spaniards lost in three days
what they spent more than three years to recover, and
spent in vain.

Though the place was taken by an English fleet, it was
not taken for England, but in the name of an Archduke
of Austria, whom England supported as a pretender to
the Spanish throne; and had he succeeded in gaining it
the place would doubtless have been turned over to him
(as on a visit to Gibraltar he was received by the garrison
as lawful sovereign of Spain, and proclaimed King by the
title of Charles III.), but as he was finally defeated, England thought it not a bad thing to keep the place for
herself.

Hardly had it slipped from their hands before the
Spaniards realized the tremendous blow which had been
given to their power and their pride, and made desperate endeavors to recover it. The very same year they
attacked it with a large army and fleet. At the beginning an attempt was made which would seem to have been
conceived in the heroism of despair. The eastern side of
Gibraltar terminates in a tremendous cliff, rising fourteen
hundred feet above the sea, which thunders against the

CATALAN BAY, ON THE EAST SIDE OF GIBRALTAR

Cliff Scaled by the Spaniards in an Attempt to Take the Rock by Surprise.

rocks below. This side has never been fortified, for the
reason that it is so defended by nature that it needs no
other defence. One would as soon think of storming El
Capitan in the valley of the Yosemite as the eastern side
of the Rock of Gibraltar. Yet he who has followed a
Swiss guide in the Alps knows that with his cool head and
agile step he will climb heights which seemed inaccessible.
And so a Spanish shepherd, or goatherd, had found a path
from Catalan Bay, up which he offered to lead a party
to the top, and five hundred men were daring enough to
follow him. They knew that the attempt was desperate,
but braced up their courage by religious enthusiasm, devot-
ing themselves to the sacrifice by taking the sacrament, and
binding themselves to capture Gibraltar or perish in the
attempt. In the darkness and silence of the night they
crept slowly upward till a part had reached the top, and
concealed themselves in St. Michael's Cave until the break
of day; when with the earliest dawn they attacked the
Signal Station, killing the guard, and then by ropes and
ladders brought up the rest of the party. Following up
the momentary success, they stormed the wall of Charles
V., so called because constructed by him. But by this
time the garrison had been awakened to the fact that there
was an enemy within the walls. The roll of drums from
below summoned the troops to arms, and soon the grenadiers came rushing up the hill. Exposed to the fire from
above, many fell, but nothing could check their advance,
and reaching the top they charged with such fury that

half of the party that had scaled the heights soon fell, some of whom were driven over the cliff into the sea. An officer who was present during the whole of the siege tells how they made short work of it. "Five hundred Spaniards attacked the Middle Hill but were soon repulsed, and two hundred men with their commanding officer taken. The rest were killed by our shot, or in making their escape broke their necks over the rocks and precipices, which in that place are many and prodigiously high."

So ended the first and last attempt to take Gibraltar in the rear. But still the Spanish army lay encamped before the town, and the siege was kept up for six months with a loss of ten thousand men. No other attack was made during that war, though the war itself raged elsewhere for seven years more, till it was closed by the treaty of Utrecht, in which Gibraltar was finally ceded to Great Britain.

But the Spaniards did not give it up yet. In 1727 they renewed the struggle, and besieged the place for five months with nearly twenty thousand men, but with the same result as before, after which it had rest and quiet for half a century, till the time of the Great Siege, which I am now to describe.

It seems beginning a long way off to find any connection between the siege of Gibraltar and the battle of Saratoga ; but one followed from the other. The surrender of General Burgoyne (who had marched from Canada with a large army to crush the Rebellion in the Colonies) was the first great event that gave hope, in the eyes of Europe, to the cause of American independence, and led France to join it openly, as she had before favored it secretly. Spain followed France, having a common hatred of England, with the special grievance of the loss of Gibraltar, which she hoped, with the help of her powerful ally, to recover.

In such a contest the chances were more evenly balanced than might be at first supposed. True, England had the advantage of possession, and if possession is nine points of the law, it is more than nine points in war, especially when the possessor is intrenched in the strongest fortress in the world. But as an offset to this, she had to hold it in an enemy's country. Gibraltar was a part of the territory of Spain, in which the English had not a foot of ground but the Rock on which they stood; while it was much nearer to France than to England. Thus the allied powers had facilities for attacking it both by land and sea, and brought against it such tremendous forces that it could not have held out for nearly four years, had it not been for the British power of resistance, animated by one of the bravest of soldiers.

To begin with, England did not commit the folly by which Spain had lost Gibraltar—in leaving it with an insufficient garrison. It had over five thousand troops in the fortress—a force by which it was thoroughly manned.

But its power for defence was doubled by having a commander, who was fitted by nature and by training for the responsibilities that were to be laid upon him. George Augustus Eliott was the son of Sir Gilbert Eliott, of Roxburghshire, where he was born in 1718. Scotch families in those days, like those of our New England fathers, were apt to be large, and the future defender of Gibraltar was one of eleven children, of whom but two were daughters, and of the nine sons George was the youngest. After such education as he could receive at home, he was sent to the continent, and entered the University of Leyden, where, with his other studies, he acquired a knowledge of German, which was to be of practical use to him afterward, as he was to serve for a year in a German army. But France was the country that then took the lead in the art of war; and from Holland he was sent to a famous military school in Picardy, founded by Vauban, the constructor of the French fortresses, where he learned the principles which he was to apply to the defence of a greater fortress than any in France. He gave particular attention also to the practice of gunnery. As Napoleon learned the art of war in the artillery school of Brienne, so did Eliott in the school of La Fère. An incidental advantage of this French education was that he acquired the language so that he could speak it fluently, a knowledge which was of service to him afterward when he had so much to do with the French, even though it were as enemies.

From France Eliott travelled into other countries on a tour of military observation, and then enlisted for a year in the Prussian army, which was considered the model in the way of discipline. Thus equipped for the life of a soldier, he returned to Scotland, where (as his father wished that he should be further inured to the practice of arms), he entered a Welsh regiment then in Edinburgh as a volunteer, and served with it for a year, from which he went into the engineer corps at Woolwich, and then into a troop of "horse grenadiers," that, under his vigorous training, became famous as a corps of heavy cavalry. When it was ordered to the Continent, he went with it, and served in Germany and the Netherlands, where he took part in several engagements and was wounded at the battle of Dettingen.

In this varied service Eliott had gained the reputation of being a brave and capable officer, but had as yet no opportunity to show the extraordinary ability which he was afterward to display. He had, however, acquired such a mastery of the art of war, that he was fitted for any position. In those days, however, promotion was slow, and he had served in the army (which he entered at the age of seventeen,) forty years, and was fifty-seven years old, and had yet reached only the grade of a Lieutenant-General, when, in 1775, he was placed in command of the fortress of Gibraltar. This was four years before the siege began, by which time he was a little turned of sixty, so that he was familiarly called "Old Eliott." But his good Scotch frame did him service now, for he was hale and strong, with a heart of oak and a frame of iron; asking no indulgence on account of his years, but ready to endure every fatigue and share every danger. Such was the man who was to conduct the defence of Gibraltar, and to be, from the beginning to the end, its very heart and soul.*

It was in the year 1779, and on the very longest day of the year, the 21st of June, that Spain, by order of the King, severed all communication with Gibraltar. But this was not war; it was simply non-intercourse, and not a hostile gun was fired for months. It is an awkward thing to strike the first blow where relations have been friendly. It had long been the custom of the Spaniards to keep a regiment of cavalry at San Roque, and one of infantry at Algeciras, across the bay, between which and the garrison there was a frequent exchange of military courtesies. Two days before this abrupt termination of

---

* The above outline is derived chiefly from Chalmers' Biographical Dictionary, a work in thirty-two octavo volumes, published in London more than seventy years ago (in 1814). I have sought for fuller information from other sources, but without result. The "Encyclopædia Britannica," in its article on Gibraltar refers to a "Life of Eliott," but I have not been able to find it either in the United States or in England. After a fruitless search in the Astor Library, with the aid of the Librarian, I cabled twice to London, the second time directing that search be made in the British Museum, but received reply that the book could not be found. The American Consul at Gibraltar writes me that he cannot find it there. Can it be possible that there is not in existence any full and authentic record of one of the greatest heroes that England has produced? Has such a man no place in English history except to furnish the subject of an article in a Biographical Dictionary?

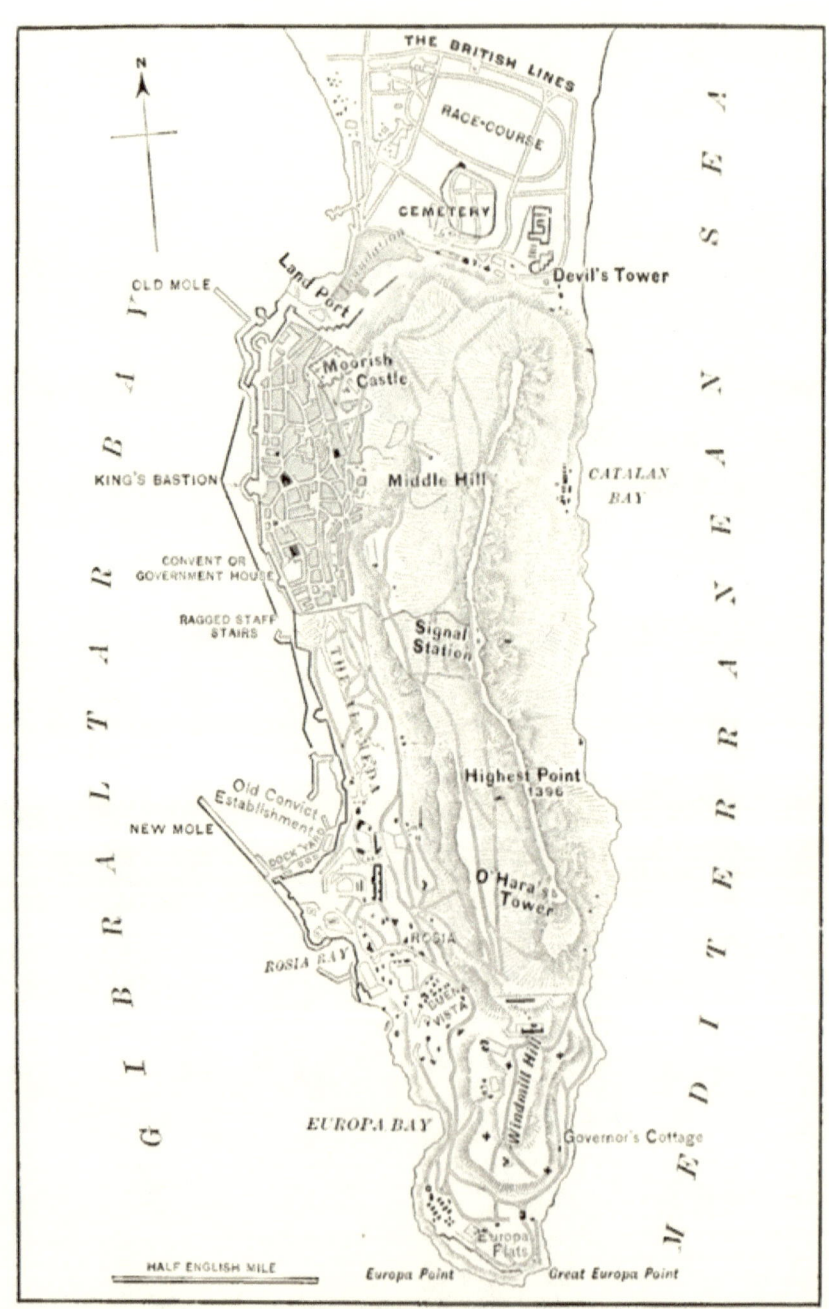

PLAN OF GIBRALTAR.

intercourse, the Governor had been to pay his respects to General Mendoza, and found him very much embarrassed by the visit, so that he suspected something was wrong, and was not surprised when the order came down from Madrid to cut off all friendly communication. The Spaniards had resolved to make a fresh attempt to recapture Gibraltar, thinking at first that it might be done by a blockade, without a bombardment. There are two ways to take a fortress—by shot and shell, or *by starvation*. The latter may be slower and not so striking to the imagination as carrying a walled city by storm, but it is even more certain of success if only the operation can be completely done. But to this end the place must be sealed up so tightly that there shall be no going out nor coming in. This seems a very simple process, but in execution is not so easy, especially if the fortress be of large extent, and has approaches by land and sea. The Spaniards began with a vigor that seemed to promise success, by constructing a parallel across the isthmus which connects the Rock with the mainland. This was itself a formidable undertaking, but they seemed not to care for cost or labor. Putting ten thousand men at work, they had in a few weeks drawn a line across the Neutral Ground, which rendered access to the garrison impossible *by land*. Any supplies must come *by sea*.

To prevent this, the Spaniards had a large fleet in the Bay and cruising in the Straits. But with all their vigilance, they found it hard to keep a blockade of a Rock,

with a circuit of seven miles, when there were hundreds
of eyes looking out from the land, answered by hundreds
of watchers from the sea. In dark nights boats with muffled oars glided between the blockading ships, and stole
up to some sheltered nook, bringing news from the outside world. And there were always daring cruisers ready
to attempt to run the blockade, taking any risk for the
sake of the large reward in case of success. Sometimes
the weather would favor them. A fierce "Levanter"
blowing from the east, would drive off the fleet, and fill
the Straits with fog and mist, under cover of which they
could run in undiscovered. At another time a bold privateer would come in, in face of the fleet, and if sighted
and pursued, would set all sail, and rush to destruction
or to victory. Once under the guns of the fortress she
was safe. Thus for a time the garrison received irregu-
lar supplies.*

But in spite of all it was often in sore and pressing
need. The soldiers required to be well fed to be fit for
duty, and yet not infrequently they were half starved.
Six thousand capacious mouths made havoc of provisions,

---

* The incidents so briefly told in the following sketch are derived chiefly from "A History of the Siege of Gibraltar," by
John Drinkwater, a Captain in the 72d Regiment, which formed
part of the garrison, and who was therefore a witness and an actor
in the scenes he describes. His narrative, though written in the
plain style of a soldier, yet being "compiled from observations
daily noted down upon the spot," is invaluable as a minute and
faithful record of one of the greatest events in modern war.

and a brig-load was quickly consumed. As if this was not enough, the hucksters of the town, who had got hold of the necessaries of life, secreted them to create an appearance of greater scarcity, that they might extort still larger prices from the famine-stricken inhabitants. Drinkwater, in his "History of the Siege," gives a list of prices actually paid.

"The hind-quarter of an Algerian sheep, with the head and tail, was sold for seven pounds and ten shillings; a large sow for upwards of twenty-nine pounds; a goat, with a young kid, the latter about twelve months old, for near twelve pounds. An English milch cow was sold for fifty guineas, reserving to the seller a pint of milk each day whilst she gave milk; and another cow was purchased by a Jew for sixty guineas, but the beast was in such a feeble condition that she dropped down dead before she had been removed many hundred yards."

But it was not only meat that was wanted: bread was so scarce that even biscuit-crumbs sold for a shilling a pound! The economy of flour was carried to the most minute details. It was an old custom that the soldiers who were to mount guard should powder their hair, like the servants in the royal household; but even this had to be denied them. The Governor would not waste a thimbleful of the precious article, which he had rather see going into the stomachs of his brave soldiers than plastered on their hair.

A brief entry in a soldier's diary, tells how the pinch came closer and closer: "Another bakery shut up to-day.

No more flour. Even salt meat scarce, and no vegetables."

Shortly after this an examination of supplies revealed
the fact that no fresh meat remained, with the exception
of an old cow, which was reserved for the sick. A goose
was sold for two pounds, and a turkey for four.

In such a condition—so near to the starvation point—
there was but one thing to do. It was a hard necessity,
but there was no help for it, and an order was issued for
the immediate reduction of the soldiers' rations, already
barely sufficient to sustain life.

The effect of this continued privation upon the *morale*
of the garrison was very depressing. Hunger, like disease, weakens the vital forces, and when both come together they weigh upon the spirit until the manliest
give way to discouragement. That this feeling did not
become general was owing chiefly to the personal influence of the Governor, whose presence was medicine to
the sick, and a new force to the well, making the brave
braver and the strong stronger. When famine stared
them in the face he made light of it, and taught others to
make light of it by sharing their privations. At the beginning of the siege he had formed a resolution to share
all the hardships of his men, even to limiting himself to
the fare of a common soldier. His food was of the plain-
est and coarsest. As a Scotch boy he had perhaps been
brought up on oatmeal porridge, and it was good enough
for him still. If a blockade-runner came in with a cargo

of fresh provisions, he did not reserve the best for himself, but all was sold in the open market. If it be said that he had the means to buy which others had not, yet his tastes were so simple that he preferred to share the soldier's mess rather than to partake of the richest food. Besides, he had a principle about it. To such extent did he carry this, that, on one occasion, when the enemy's commander, as a courtesy not unusual in war, sent him a present of fruit, vegetables, and game, the Governor, while returning a polite acknowledgment, begged that the act might not be repeated, for that he had a fixed resolution "never to receive or procure, by any means whatever, any provisions or other commodity for his own private use;" adding, "I make it a point of honor to partake both of plenty and scarcity in common with the lowest of my brave fellow-soldiers." Once indeed when the stress was the sharpest, he showed his men how close they could come to starvation and not die, by living eight days on four ounces of rice a day! The old hero had been preparing for just such a crisis as this by his previous life, for he had trained himself from boyhood to bear every sort of hardship and privation. The argument for total abstinence needs no stronger fact to support it than that the defence of Gibraltar was conducted by a man who needed no artificial stimulus to keep up his courage or brace his nerves against the shock of battle. "Old Eliott," the brave Scotchman and magnificent soldier, was able to stand to his guns with nothing stronger to fire his

blood than cold water. Chalmers' Biographical Dictionary says:

"He was perhaps the most abstemious man of the age. His
food was vegetables, and his drink water. He neither indulged
himself in animal food nor wine. He never slept more than four
hours at a time, so that he was up later and earlier than most other
men. He had so inured himself to habits of hardness, that the
things which are difficult and painful to other men were to him
his daily practice, and rendered pleasant by use. It could not be
easy to starve such a man into a surrender, nor to surprise him.
His wants were easily supplied, and his watchfulness was beyond
precedent. The example of the commander-in-chief in a besieged
garrison, has a most persuasive efficacy in forming the manners of
the soldiery. Like him, his brave followers came to regulate
their lives by the most strict rules of discipline before there arose
a necessity for so doing ; and severe exercise, with short diet, became habitual to them by their own choice."

Thus the old Governor, by starving himself, taught his
men how to bear starvation. After that a soldier, however pinched, would hardly dare to complain.

He might not indeed care for himself, but he could not
help caring for those dependent on him. The cruel hardship of it was that the suffering fell not on the soldiers
alone, but on women and children. The Governor had
tried, as far as possible, to send away all non-combatants.
But it was not always easy to separate families. There
were soldiers' wives, who clung to their husbands all the
more because of their danger. If a Scotch grenadier
were to have his legs carried off by a cannon-ball, or
frightfully torn by a shell, who could nurse him so well as
his faithful wife, who had followed him in the camp and

in the field ? And so, for better, for worse, many a wife, with the courage of womanhood, determined to share her husband's fate. It was a brave resolution, but it only involved them in the common distress. There were so many more mouths to feed, when the supply even for the soldiers was all too little. The captain who has recorded so faithfully the heroisms and the privations of the siege, says:

"Many officers and soldiers had families to support out of the pittance received from the victualling office. A soldier and his wife and three children would inevitably have been starved to death had not the generous contribution of his corps relieved his family. One woman actually died through want, and many were so enfeebled that it was not without great attention they recovered. Thistles, dandelions, and wild leeks were for some time the daily nourishment of numbers."

Another account tells the same pitiful tale, with additional horrors :

"The ordinary means of sustenance were now almost exhausted, and *roots and weeds*, with thistles and wild onions, were greedily sought after and devoured by the famished inhabitants.

"Bread was becoming so scarce that the daily rations were served out under protection of a guard, and the weak, the aged, and the infirm, who could not struggle against the hungry, impetuous crowd that thronged the doors of the bakeries, often returned to their homes robbed of their share : " *

"Ancell's Journal," kept during the siege, thus records the impressions of the day:

"It is a terribly painful sight to see the fighting among the people for a morsel of bread at an exorbitant price ; men wrestling, women entreating, and children crying, a jargon of all lan-

* Sayer's History of Gibraltar, pp. 297, 298.

guages, piteously pouring forth their complaints. You would think sensibility would shed a tear, and yet when we are in equal distress ourselves our feelings for others rather subside."

While this slow and wasting process of starvation was going on, the garrison were in a fearful state of suspense. Sometimes it seemed as if England had forgotten them, but again came tidings that the nation was watching their defence with the utmost anxiety, and would speedily send relief. The time of waiting seemed long as the months passed—summer and autumn and part of winter, and no help appeared. The blockade began in June, 1779, and it was January, 1780, before the fleet of Admiral Rodney, after gaining a battle over the Spanish fleet off the coast of Portugal, bore away to the south. To those who were watching from the top of the Rock, probably no event of their lives ever moved them so much as when they first caught sight of the English ships entering the Straits of Gibraltar. Men, women, and children, wept aloud for joy, for the coming fleet brought them life from the dead. And when it anchored in the bay, and the ships began to unload, they brought forth not only guns and ammunition, but more priceless treasures—beef, pork, butter, flour, peas, oatmeal, raisins, and biscuits, as well as coals, iron hoops, and candles! Revelling in such abundance, could they ever want again? It was indeed a timely relief, and if the fleet could have remained, it might have put an end to the siege. But England was then carrying on wars in two hemispheres; and while the

French fleet was crossing the Atlantic to aid the American colonies in gaining their independence, she could not afford that her largest fleet should lie idle in the Bay of Gibraltar. As soon, therefore, as the stores could be landed, Admiral Rodney returned to England. The Governor seized the opportunity to send home great numbers of invalids and women. It was necessary that the garrison should "strip for the fight," as there were darker days to come.

Gibraltar had been saved from the jaws of famine by the arrival of the English fleet. But as soon as it left, the Spanish ships remained masters of the bay, and the blockade was closer than ever. The garrison had had a narrow escape. That it might not be caught so again, the Governor, with his Scotch thrift, put his men upon a new kind of service, quite apart from military duty. The Rock is not wholly barren. There are many nooks and corners that are bright with flowers, and anything that the earth can yield will ripen under that warm southern sky. Accordingly the soldiers, in the intervals of firing the big guns, were put to do a little gardening; and turned patches of ground here and there to cultivation; and where the hillside was too steep, the earth was raised into terraces and banked up with walls, on which they raised small quantities of lettuce or cabbages; so that afterward, although they still suffered for many of the comforts, if not the necessaries, of life, they never came quite so near absolute starvation.

This "home produce" was the more important as the garrison was now to be cut off from its principal resource outside. For a time it had been able to obtain supplies from the Barbary Coast. At first the Moors were all on the side of England, for the Spaniards were their hereditary enemies, who had fought them for hundreds of years, and finally driven them out of Spain, for which the Moors took a pious revenge by thronging the mosques of Tangier to pray that Allah would give the victory to the arms of England! But after a time they saw things in a new light. It could not be Christian charity that softened their hearts toward their old enemies, for they hated the very name of Christian, but some secret influence (was it Spanish gold?) so worked on the mind of the Sultan of Morocco that he became convinced that Allah was on the side of the besiegers—a discovery which he announced in a manner that was not quite in the usual style of diplomatic intercourse. Thus, without any warning,

"A party of black troops that were quartered in the vicinity of Tangier, came to the house of the British Consul, and being introduced, informed him that they had orders from their master to abuse and insult him in the grossest manner, which they immediately put in execution by spitting in his face, seizing him by the collar, and threatening to stab him with their daggers!"

Fortunately he escaped with nothing worse than this gross outrage; but the serious part of the business was that it cut off all communication of Gibraltar with the Barbary Coast; for the Sultan prohibited the export of

provisions, and as the supplies brought by the convoy
were exhausted in a few months, the garrison was again,
not indeed at the starvation point, but in sore need
of what was for its health and vigor. The meagre diet
threatened to produce a pestilence. At one time there
were seven hundred men in the hospitals; at another the
small-pox broke out; and at another the garrison was so
reduced by the scurvy, caused by the use of salt meats,
that strong men became weak as children, and hobbled
about on crutches. This threatened a great disaster,
which was averted only by lemons! In the moment of
extremity a Dutch "dogger" coming from Malaga was
captured, and found to be laden with oranges and lemons,
"a freight which, at such a crisis, was of more value to
the garrison than tons of powder or magazines of ammunition." The lemons were instantly distributed in the
hospitals. The men seized them and devoured them
ravenously, and the restoration was so speedy as to seem
almost miraculous.

And yet this relief was only temporary. Soon we
have this picture of the condition of the garrison:

"As the spring of 1781 advanced, the situation assumed the
most distressing aspect. The few provisions which remained were
bad in quality, and having been kept too long were decomposed
and uneatable. The most common necessaries of life were exor-
bitantly dear; bad ship biscuit, full of worms, was sold at a shilling a pound; flour, in not much better condition, at the same
price; old dried peas, a shilling and fourpence; salt, half dirt,
the sweepings of ships' bottoms and storehouses, at eight pence;
old salt butter, at two shillings and sixpence; and English far-

thing candles cost sixpence apiece. Fresh provisions commanded a still higher price: turkeys sold at three pounds twelve shillings, sucking pigs at two guineas, and a guinea was refused for a calf's pluck.

"The English government, aware of this condition of things, had for months turned their attention to the relief of the fortress; but the many exigencies of the war, and the extensive arena over which it was spread, caused so many demands upon the navy that it had hitherto been impossible to provide a fleet for the succor of Gibraltar. But the relief of the garrison was indispensable, and the honor of England required that it should be executed. Accordingly the government made extraordinary efforts to equip a squadron to convoy a flotilla of merchantmen to the Rock." *

But with all their efforts, it was more than a year before the second fleet arrived. When it came, it was loaded with all conceivable supplies, which took ten days to unload. The joy of the beleaguered garrison knew no bounds. And yet this new relief only precipitated a calamity which had been long impending. The scene of the arrival is thus described by an eye-witness:

"At daybreak, April 12th, the much-expected fleet, under the command of Admiral Darby, was in sight from our Signal-house, but was not discernible from below, being obscured by a thick mist. As the sun, however, became more powerful, the fog gradually rose, like the curtain of a vast theatre, discovering to the anxious garrison one of the most beautiful and pleasing scenes it is possible to conceive. The convoy, consisting of near a hundred vessels, led by several men-of-war, their sails just enough filled for steerage; whilst the majority of the line-of-battle ships lay-to under the Barbary shore, having orders not to enter the bay lest the enemy should molest them with their fire-ships. The ecstasies of the inhabitants at this grand and exhilarating sight

* Sayer's History of Gibraltar, pp. 346, 347.

are not to be described. Their expressions of joy far exceeded their former exultations [at the arrival of the fleet under Admiral Rodney]. Alas! they little dreamed of the tremendous blow that impended, which was to annihilate their property, and reduce many of them to indigence and beggary." *

What this blow was, at once appeared. The arrival of the second fleet from England convinced the Spaniards that it would be impossible to reduce Gibraltar by blockade, and determined them to try the other alternative of bombardment. Enormous batteries, mounting 170 guns and 80 mortars, had been planted along the shore; and now (before even the English ships could be unladen of their stores) was opened all round the bay a *feu d'enfer*, which was kept up for six weeks! Only two hours out of the twenty-four was there any cessation, and that for a singular reason. National customs must rule in war as in peace. The Spaniards began their fire at daybreak, and continued it without intermission till noon. Then suddenly it ceased, and the camp of the besiegers relapsed into silence: for that the officers, if not the men, *were asleep!* What Spanish gentleman could be deprived of his *siesta?* At two o'clock precisely they woke up and went to fighting again. At nightfall the cannon ceased, but only that the mortars (which did not need to be aimed with precision, and therefore could be fired in darkness as well as in daylight) opened their larger throats, and kept up the roar till daybreak. Thus, with only the time

* Drinkwater, p. 68.

of the *siesta*, there was not an hour of day or night that the Rock did not echo with tremendous reverberations. The town was soon set on fire, and completely destroyed. There was no safety anywhere, not even in the casemates. If a bomb-proof withstood a falling shell, it would sometimes explode at the open door, wounding those within. Men were killed sleeping in their beds. The scene at night was more terrible than by day, as the shells were more clearly seen in their deadly track. Sometimes a dozen would be wheeling in the air at the same moment, keeping every eye strained to see where the bolts would fall, and the bravest held their breath when (as was several times the case) they fell near the powder magazines!

Again, the soldiers were not the only ones to suffer: their wives and children were their partners in misery. When the town was on fire, the people fled from it, and at a distance watched the flames that rose from their burning dwellings, in which all their little property was consumed—the roofs that sheltered them, and even the food that fed them. For six weeks they had not a moment's rest, day nor night. Although they had fled to the southern end of the Rock, destruction pursued them there. The Spanish ships had a custom of sailing round Europa Point, and firing indiscriminately on shore. This was generally at night, so that the poor creatures who had lain down to snatch a moment of forgetfulness, were roused at midnight and fled almost naked to seek for shelter behind rocks and in holes in the ground, in which they cowered like hunted beasts, till the storm of fire had passed over them.

The troops were not quite so badly off, for though they were shelled out of their old quarters, and had not a roof to cover them, yet English soldiers and sailors are ingenious, and getting hold of some old ship canvas they rigged up a few forlorn tents, which they pitched on the hillside. But again they were discomfited. Gibraltar is subject at certain seasons to terrific storms of thunder and lightning, and now the rains poured down the side of the Rock in such floods as to sweep away the tents, and leave the men exposed to the fury of the elements. It seemed as if the stars in their courses fought against them. But they were to find that the stars in their courses fight for those who fight for themselves.

Sometimes the storms, so terrible in one way, brought relief in another. There had been a scarcity of fuel as well as of food. A soldier could hardly pick up sticks to make his pot boil, and cook his scanty meal; so that when a furious gale wrecked a ship in the bay, and cast its fragments on the shore, which furnished fuel for their camp-fires for some weeks, they counted it a providential interposition for their deliverance; and as the firelight cast its ruddy glow in their faces, they thanked God and took courage.

But with all their courage, kept up by such occasional good fortune, it was a life-and-death struggle, as they fought not only with the enemy, but with hunger and cold, and every form of privation.

During all this dreadful time the old Governor was magnificent. Going among the families that were houseless and homeless, for whom he felt the utmost sympathy (for with all his rugged strength he had a very tender heart), he allayed their fears; terrified and miserable as they were, it was impossible to resist the sunshine of that kindly Scotch face.*

Then he turned to his soldiers, who may well have

---

* It is a common saying that the brave are generous, but this is not always so. Some of the bravest men that ever lived have been cold-hearted and cruel. But Eliott, though he had an iron frame and iron will, was as soft-hearted as a woman. Nothing roused his indignation more than an act of inhumanity on the part of a superior toward an inferior. Hence he was the protector not only of women and children, but of prisoners who fell into his hands, and who might otherwise be exposed to the license of soldiers demoralized by victory. He repressed all pillage and stood between the victors and the vanquished, as the defender of the defenceless. So noted was he for his humanity that those who were in trouble sought his protection, and his response to their appeals sometimes took them by surprise. An amusing illustration of this occurred some years before at the capture of Havana: A Frenchman who had suffered greatly by the depredations of the soldiery, came to him, and begged in bad English that he would interfere to have his property restored. But his wife, who was a woman of high spirit, was angry at her husband that he should ask any favor of an enemy, and turned to him sharply, saying, "Comment pouvez vous demander de grace à un homme qui vient vous dépouiller ? N'en esperez pas." The husband persisting in his application, the wife grew more loud in her censure, and said, "Vous n'êtes pas Français!" The General, who was busy writing at the time, overheard the conversation, and as he spoke French perfectly, turned to the woman, and said smiling, "Madame, ne vous échauffez pas ; ce que votre mari demande lui sera accordé." At this she broke out again, as if it were the last degree of indignity, that the Englishman should speak French : "Oh, faut-il pour surcroît de malheur, que le barbare parle Français !" The General was so much pleased with the woman's spirit that he not only procured them their property again, but also took pains to accommodate them in every respect.—*Chalmers' Biographical Dictionary.*

been appalled by the tremendous fire, which wrought such wreck and ruin. If they were troubled and anxious, he was calm. He shunned no danger, as he had shunned no privation. Indeed danger did not affect him as it did other men, but only roused the lion in his breast. The more the danger grew, the higher rose his unconquerable spirit. He was constantly under fire, and his perfect coolness tended to produce the same composure in others equally exposed. Terrible as the bombardment was, not for one moment did he admit the possibility of surrender.

But now came a new danger, not from without, but from within. The fire which swept the town uncovered cellars and other hiding-places in which the hucksters had concealed provisions and other stores to double their price, and extort the last penny from the half-fed population. When their storehouses were destroyed little sympathy was felt for them. Indeed, there was a general feeling of savage exultation; and as here and there supplies of food were found, they were seized without scruple and appropriated to the common use. Men who have been living on short allowance are apt to be led into excesses by sudden plenty, and the soldiers could hardly be blamed if for once they gave themselves a generous supply. From the extreme of want they went to the extreme of waste. In some cases incredible profusion prevailed. Drinkwater says: "Among other instances of caprice and extravagance, I recollect seeing a party of soldiers roast a pig by a fire made of cinnamon!"

If this had been all, there would not have been so much
to regret.   But in the stores were casks of wine and bar-
rels of spirits, which were now knocked on the head, and
the contents distributed with no restraint, till soon a large
part of the garrison was in such a state of intoxication as
to be utterly unfit for duty.   "As the enemy's shells
forced open the secret recesses of the merchants, the soldiers instantly availed themselves of the opportunity to
seize upon the liquors, which they conveyed to haunts of
their own.   Here in parties they barricaded their quarters
against all opposers, and insensible of their danger, re-
galed themselves with the spoils."   For a time this sudden madness ran riot in the streets, threatening the over-
throw of all order and discipline.

It can hardly be matter of surprise that the reaction
from this long tension of feeling, with the sudden temptation to drunkenness, should show itself in wild extrava-
gances.   An incident related in " Ancell's Journal," shows
the soldier in the mood of making sport of his dangers:

"April 15, 1781.—Yesterday I met a soldier singing in the
street with uncommon glee, notwithstanding the enemy were firing with prodigious warmth,

> 'A soldier's life is a merry life,
>   From care and trouble free.'

He ran to me with eagerness, and presenting his bottle, cried:
'D——n me if I don't like fighting, with plenty of good liquor
for carrying away. 'Why, Jack,' says I, 'what have you been
about?' 'Faith,' says he, 'I scarce know myself. I have been

constantly on foot and watch, half-starved and without money, facing a parcel of pitiful Spaniards. I have been fighting, wheeling, marching, counter-marching, sometimes with a firelock, sometimes with a handspike, and now with my bottle.'

"A shell that instant burst, a piece of which knocked the bottle out of his hand. 'Jack,' says I, 'are you not thankful to God for your preservation?' 'How do you mean?' says he; 'fine talking of God with a soldier whose trade and occupation is cutting throats. Divinity and slaughter sound very well together; they jingle like a cracked bell in the hands of a noisy crier. My religion is a firelock, open touch-hole, good flint, well-rammed charge, and seventy rounds: this is military creed. Come, comrade, drink!'"

Such license as this would soon demoralize the best troops in the world. Had the Spaniards known the degree to which it existed at that moment, and been able to effect an entrance into the fortress, Gibraltar might have been lost.

The insubordination was suppressed only by the most strenuous efforts of the Governor and the vigorous enforcement of discipline. An order was issued that any soldier caught marauding should be "executed *immediately*," and this summary judgment was put in force in several cases, where men were not only executed without a moment's delay, but on the very spot where the crime was committed. This timely severity, with the personal influence of the Governor, at length brought the soldiers to their senses, and order was restored. Perhaps they were brought back to duty in part by the continued roar of that terrific bombardment, for in a true soldier nothing rouses the martial spirit like the sound of the enemy's

guns. Danger and duty go together: and many of those
who had been carried away by this temporary frenzy,
when they "came to themselves," were among the bravest who fought in the conflicts that were yet to come.

It was now a struggle of endurance—firing and coun-
ter-firing month after month, with exciting incidents now
and then to relieve the monotony of the siege. Of these
episodes the most notable was the sortie executed on the
night of November 26, 1781. The siege had lasted more
than two years, and the Spaniards, boastful and confident
as they are apt to be, by this time appreciated the enormous difficulty of attacking the Rock of Gibraltar. To do
them justice, instead of being daunted by the greatness of
the task, their military ardor rose with the vastness of the
undertaking, and they had been engaged for months in
rearing a stupendous parallel across the Neutral Ground,
to be mounted with the heaviest battering artillery. The
Governor had kept his eye upon the progress of the work,
and as he saw its lines spreading out wider and wider,
and rising higher and higher, he could not but feel anxiety for the moment when these batteries should open, and
rain shot and shell upon the devoted garrison. The way
in which he met the new danger showed that he had the
promptness in action of a great commander.

From the beginning of the siege he had observed the
utmost economy in the use of his resources. He was
sparing of his ammunition, and sometimes reproached his
officers with great severity for wasting it in unimportant

attacks. He saved his powder as he saved his men. Indeed he was sparing of everything except himself. Yet "he never relaxed from his discipline by the appearance of security, nor hazarded the lives of his garrison by wild experiments. Collected within himself, he in no instance destroyed, by premature attacks, the labors which would cost the enemy time, patience, and expense to complete; he deliberately observed their approaches, and seized on the proper moment in which to make his attack with success." For months he had been waiting and watching: the time for action had now come.

During the siege there had been frequent desertions on both sides. Now and then soldiers of the garrison, wearied with the interminable siege (and thinking it better to take the chances of instant death than to be shut up in a fortress-prison and perish by inches), let themselves down by ropes over the face of the Rock. Some escaped to the enemy, and some were dashed on the rocks below. On the other side there were among the Spanish soldiers a good many Walloons from Belgium, who had no interest in the contest, and were as ready to fight on one side as the other. Occasionally one of these would stray out of the camp, as if without intention, and when he had got at a distance which he thought gave him a chance of escape, would take to his heels and run for the gates of the fortress. If discovered, he was immediately fired at, and a mounted guard started in pursuit, and if overtaken, he was brought back, and the next day his body, hanging from the scaffold, in full sight of the Rock, served as a ghastly warning alike to the besiegers and the besieged.

But, in spite of all, desertions went on. One day a couple of deserters were brought to the Governor, one of whom proved to be uncommonly intelligent, and gave important information. "Old Eliott" took him up to a point of the Rock from which they could look down into the camp of the besiegers, and questioned him minutely as to its condition and the intentions of the enemy. He said that the parallel was nearly completed; and that as soon as all was ready the Spaniards would make a grand assault; but that meanwhile the works, enormous as they were, were not guarded by a large force, the besiegers not dreaming that the batteries prepared for attack could be themselves attacked! The Governor instantly perceived the value of this information, but kept it to himself, and had the deserter closely confined lest he should incautiously reveal to others what he had told to him. Keeping his own counsel, he made his preparations, which he did not disclose even to his lieutenants until the moment for action. It was in the evening when he called them together, and announced his intention to make an attack on the works of the besiegers *that very night*, and at midnight about two thousand men were in arms on the " Red Sands," now the Alameda, to carry the daring purpose into execution. Their orders were of the strictest kind: " Each man to have thirty-six rounds of ammunition, with a good flint in his piece and another in his pocket. No drums to go out, excepting two with each of the regiments. *No volunteers will be allowed*." The brave old commander wanted no amateurs on such an occasion. "No person to advance before the front, unless ordered by the officer commanding the column : and *the most profound silence to be observed*." As it took two or three hours to form the columns, and acquaint all with the special duty to be undertaken, and the necessity for the strictest obedience, it was nearly three o'clock when they began to move. The moon was just setting across the bay, and soon all was dark and still, as the men advanced with quick but cautious steps through the silent streets. The commander had picked his men for the daring attempt. Knowing how powerful are the traditions of bravery, he had chosen two regiments that had fought side by side at the battle of Minden, twenty-two years before. The officers to lead them he had chosen with equal care, and yet, when it came to the moment of action, the old soldier felt such a fire in his bones that he could not resist the impulse to keep them company. As they emerged from the gates they had still three-quarters of a mile across the plain to reach the enemy's works. With all the precautions to secure silence, the tramp of two thousand men, however muffled, could not but reach the ears of the Spanish sentinels, and a few rapid shots told that they were discovered. But the alarm was given too late. It only quickened the advance of the column, which, as it reached the works, rushed over the parapet, bayoneting the men, such as did not flee, panic-stricken by the sudden attack, and spiking the guns. As the soldiers had come prepared with faggots for the purpose, they immediately set the works on fire. But even at this moment of terror there was one who thought of mercy as well as of victory. Before the flames had spread the Governor, "anxious that none of the wounded should by any accident perish in the burning batteries, went into the trench himself and found among the bodies of the slain a wounded officer, whom by his uniform he knew to be a captain of the Spanish artillery, to whom he spoke with all kindness, and promising him every assistance, ordered him to be removed, as the fire was now rapidly spreading to the spot where he lay. But the Spaniard, raising himself with difficulty, feebly exclaimed, "No, sir, no, leave me and let me perish amid the ruins of my post." In a few minutes he expired. It was afterward found that he had commanded the guard of the San Carlos battery, and that when his men threw down their arms and fled, he rushed forward into the attacking column, exclaiming, "At least one Spaniard shall die honorably," and fell where he was found, at the foot of his post." *

It was now too late to talk of mercy. In an hour the flames had spread into a conflagration that could not be subdued. As it rose into the air, it lighted up the Rock above and the plain below. Leaving the elements to com-

* Sayer's History, p. 365.

plete the work of destruction, the assailants made their
retreat, only to hear, as they re-entered the gates, the explosion of the magazines. So vast was the ruin wrought
that the camp was like a city on fire, and continued to
burn for four days, without an effort on the part of the
Spaniards (who seemed to be stunned and bewildered by
the sudden attack) to subdue the flames. Thus was destroyed at a single stroke what it had cost months of
labor and millions of money to construct.

And so the game of war went on for three long years,
until it had fixed the gaze of the whole civilized world.
The last act was to be inaugurated by a change in the
military command, and in the method of attack. Hitherto the siege had been conducted chiefly by the Spaniards, as was fitting, since, if the fortress were taken, to
Spain would fall the splendid prize. They had fought
bravely, maintaining the reputation which had never been
shaken from the days of Alva, when the Spanish infantry
was more dreaded than any other on the battle-fields of
Europe. During the siege the officers of the garrison, as
they looked down from their heights into the hostile
camp, could not but admire the way in which both officers
and men exposed themselves. It was not to their dis-
honor if they had failed in attempting the impossible.
But having to confess defeat, it was but military prudence to see if another mode of operation might not be
more successful. Accordingly, French skill in the art of
war was now called in to take part in the tremendous con-

flict. The Duc de Crillon, who had recently distinguished himself by the capture of Minorca, was put in command of the combined land forces; while a French engineer, the Chevalier d'Arçon, was to prepare an armament more formidable than had ever been known in naval warfare.

The plan had certainly the merit of boldness. There was to be no more long blockade, and no more attempt to take the place by stratagem. Gibraltar was to be taken, if at all, by hard fighting. But the conditions of battle were unequal: for how could wooden ships be matched against stone walls? No ships of the day could stand an hour against guns fired from behind those ramparts. But this engineer was bold enough to believe that vessels could be made so strong that they would withstand even that tremendous fire. He proposed to construct "battering ships" of such enormous strength that they could be moored within short range, when he in turn would open a fire equally tremendous, that should blow Gibraltar into the air! All he asked was that his flotilla might be laid close alongside the enemy, when, gun to gun and man to man, the contest should be decided. Once let him get near enough to make a breach for a storming party to mount the walls, and his French grenadiers would do the rest. It was bravely conceived, and to the day of battle it seemed as if it might be bravely done.

To begin with, ten of the largest ships in the Spanish navy were to be sacrificed: for it seemed like a sacrifice to cut down the huge bulwarks of their towering sides.

But show was to be sacrificed to strength. The new constructor would have no more three-deckers, nor two-deckers. All he wanted was one broad deck, reaching the whole length of the ship, from stem to stern, which should be as solid as if it were a part of the mainland, or a floating island, on which he could plant his guns as on the ramparts of a fortress. Having thus dismantled and razeed the great ships, he proceeded to reconstruct them without and within. His method is of interest, as showing how a hundred years ago a naval engineer anticipated the modern construction of ironclads. His battering ships were in outward shape almost exactly what the Merrimac was in our civil war. He did everything except case them with iron, the art of rolling plates of wrought iron, such as are now used in the construction of ships, not being then known. But if they could not be "plated" with iron on the outside, they were "backed" by ribs of oak within. Inside their enormous hulls was a triple thickness of beams, braced against the sides. Next to this was a layer of *sand*, in which it was supposed a cannon-ball would bury itself as in the earth. To this sand-bank, resting against its oaken backing, there was still an inner lining in a thick wall of *cork*, which, yielding like india-rubber, would offer the best resistance to the penetration of shot.

Having thus protected the hulls, it was only necessary to protect the crews. For this the decks were roofed with heavy timbers, which were covered with *ropes*, and

7

next with *hides*, after the manner of the ancient Romans; so that the men working at the guns were almost as secure from the enemy's fire as if they were inside of the strongest casemates that the art of fortification could construct. Thus shielded above and below—from the deck to the keel—these novel ships-of-war were in truth floating fortresses, and it was hardly presumptuous in their constructor to say that they "could not be burnt, nor sunk, nor taken."

These preparations for attack could not be made without the knowledge of the garrison. From the top of the Rock they had but to turn their glasses across the bay, and they could see distinctly hundreds of workmen swarming over the great hulks, and could almost hear the sound of the hammers that ceased not day nor night. Turning to the camp of the besiegers, they could see "long strings of mules streaming hourly into the trenches laden with shot, shell, and ammunition." Deserters brought in reports of the vast preparations, and the confidence they inspired. The fever of expectation had spread to the capitals of Spain and France. The King of Spain was almost beside himself with eagerness and impatience. Every morning his first question was " Is it taken?" and when answered in the negative he always kept up his courage by saying, " It will soon be ours." His expectations seemed now likely to be realized. All felt that at last the end was nigh, and the Comte d'Artois, the brother of Louis XVI., the King of France, had made the journey all the way from Paris to be present at the grand culmination of the surrender of Gibraltar!

So sure were the allies of victory that they debated among themselves as to "how many hours" the garrison could keep up a resistance. Twenty-four hours was the limit, and when the French commander, less sanguine than the naval constructors and engineers, thought it might be even *two weeks* before the place fell, he was the subject of general ridicule.

Taking for granted that the fire of the garrison would soon be silenced, precise directions were given about the landing of the storming party. As soon as a break was made, the grenadiers were to mount the walls. It was especially ordered that strong bodies of troops should *advance rapidly and cut off the retreat* of the garrison, which might otherwise flee to the heights of the Rock, and keep up for a while longer the hopeless resistance. The victory must be complete.

On the other hand, the garrison was roused to greater exertion by the greater danger. Its ardor was excited also by what was passing in other parts of the world. War was still raging in both hemispheres, with the usual vicissitudes of victory and defeat. England had lost America, but her wounded pride was soon relieved, if not entirely removed, by a great victory at sea. Cornwallis surrendered at Yorktown, in October, 1781, and only six months after, in April, 1782, Admiral Rodney (the same who had relieved Gibraltar only two years before) gained

a victory in the West Indies over Count de Grasse, which
almost annihilated the French fleet, and assured to England, whatever her losses upon land, the mastery of the
seas. The tidings of this great victory reached Gibraltar,
and fired the spirit of every Briton. The Governor was
now sixty-four years old, and the events of the last three
years might well make him feel that he was a hundred.
But his youth returned in the great crisis that was upon
him. Both Governor and garrison burned to do something worthy the name and fame of Old England. The
opportunity soon came.

Though the battering ships were regarded as invinci-
ble, yet to make assurance doubly sure the French and
Spanish fleets had been quadrupled in force. If any
man's heart had been trembling before, it must have
failed him on September 12, 1782, when there sailed
into the bay thirty-nine ships of the line, raising the
naval armament to fifty line-of-battle ships, with in-
numerable smaller vessels—the largest naval armament
since the Spanish Armada—supported on land by an
army of forty thousand men, whose batteries, mounted with the heaviest ordnance, stretched along the shore.

Against this mighty array of force by land and sea the
English commander, mustering every gun and every man,
could oppose only ninety-six pieces of artillery, manned
by seven thousand soldiers and sailors.

As the allied forces had been waiting only for the fleet,
the attack was announced for the following day, and ac-

cordingly soon after the sun rose the next morning the
battering-ships were seen to be getting under way. It
was a grand sight, at which the spirits of the besiegers
rose to the highest pitch. So confident were they of victory that thousands of spectators, among whom were
many of the Spanish nobility, had gathered near the
"Queen's Seat," in the Spanish lines, to witness the final
capture of Gibraltar, for which they had been waiting
three long years.

Even the Englishmen who lined the ramparts could not
but admire the order in which the ships took up their po-
sitions. So confident was the Spanish Admiral that they
were shot-proof and bomb-proof, that he took no pains
to keep at long range, but advanced boldly and moored
within half gunshot, with large boats full of men ready to
land as soon as the guns of the fortress were silenced.
To both sides it was evident that the decisive day had come.

While the ships were being ranged in line of battle, the
English stood at their guns in silence till "Old Eliott"
took his stand on the King's Bastion, and gave the signal
for the roar of earth and hell to begin. Instantly the
floating batteries answered from the whole line, and their
fire was taken up along the shores of the bay, till there
were four hundred guns playing on the devoted town. No
thunderstorm in the tropics ever shot out such lightnings
and thunderings. As the hills echoed the tremendous reverberations, it seemed as if the solid globe was reeling
under the shock of an earthquake.

The ships at first aimed their guns a little too high, so that balls and shells flew over the line-wall and fell in the rear; but they soon got the range, and lowering their guns to almost a dead-level, fired point-blank. "About noon their firing was powerful and well-directed." Guns were dismounted, and the wounded began to fall and to be carried to the rear. But others took their place at the guns, and kept up the steady fire, never turning from the one object directly in front. Although the batteries on the land tried to divert their fire, the Governor disdained to answer them with a single gun. "Not there! not there!" was the danger. His keen eye saw that the fate of Gibraltar was to be decided that day by the answer given to those battering ships that were pouring such a terrific fire into his lines. In the midst of it all he was as cool as if on parade. A large part of the day he kept his place on the King's Bastion, the centre at which the enemy's fire was directed, and his presence had an inspiring effect upon his men. To do them justice, the soldiers, who had served under such a commander for three years, were worthy of their leader. As he looked along the lines they were wrapped in a cloud of smoke, and yet now and then, by the flashing of the guns, he could see their heroic features glowing "with the light of battle in their faces." On that day, as with Nelson twenty-three years later, "England expected every man to do his duty," and did not expect in vain.

But for a time all their courage and skill seemed to be without result. For hours the battle raged with doubtful issue. Though the English fired at such short range, they did not produce much effect. Their thirty-two-pound shot could not pierce the thick-ribbed sides of the battering-ships, while their heaviest shells were seen to rebound from the roofs, as the shots of the Congress and the Cumberland rebounded from the roof of the Merrimac. Apparently the fire of the garrison produced as little impression on the ships as the fire of the ships produced on the rocks of Gibraltar.

The disparity of forces was so great that the allies might have carried the day if that inequality had not been balanced by one advantage of the besieged. They had one means of destruction which could not be so easily turned against land defences—in the use of hot shot. The experiment had been tried on the works of the besiegers, and they now hoped it would have still greater effect upon the ships. But their enemies were neither surprised nor daunted by this new mode of attack. They were fully aware of what the English had done, and what they proposed to do, and with true Castilian pride laughed at this new method of destruction. So much did they despise it, that one of the Spanish commanders said "he would engage to receive in his breast all the hot shot of the enemy."

Meanwhile "Old Eliott" had gone on with his preparations. A few days before, coal had been served out to the

furnaces, which had been placed beside the batteries.
These were now kept at white heat, and the heavy balls
dropped into them till they glowed like molten iron, and
then were carefully lifted to the guns.*

As the artillerymen sighted their guns they observed
with grim satisfaction that the ships had anchored at
the right distance, so that they had but to elevate their
guns *very slightly,* just enough to save the necessity of
ramming the ball with a second wadding to hold it in
place; and thus not a moment was lost when moments
were very precious, but the ball was simply rolled into the
cannon's mouth, from which it was instantly hurled at the
foe.

Yet even the hot shot did not at first make much impression. The French engineer had guarded against
them by having pumps constantly pouring water into the
layer of sand below, where a red-hot cannon-ball would
soon be rendered harmless. In fact, a number of times
during the day smoke was seen to issue from the floating
batteries, showing that the hot shot had taken effect, but
the flames were promptly extinguished. It was not till
late in the afternoon that they began to burst out, and it
was seen that the Admiral's ship was on fire. As the

---

* "The shot were heated either in the grates and furnaces made for that
purpose, or by piling them in a corner of some old house adjoining the batteries, and surrounding them with faggots, pieces of timber, and small coal."
Afterwards "the engineers erected kilns (similar to those used in burning
lime, but smaller) in various parts of the garrison. They were large enough
to heat upwards of one hundred balls in an hour and a quarter."—*Drinkwater.*

night drew on the flames became more visible, showing the exact position of the Spanish line, and furnishing a mark for the English guns. On another ship the fires advanced so rapidly that they had to flood the magazine for fear of an explosion. Others threw up rockets, and hoisted signals of distress to their consorts, and boats were seen rowing toward them. At midnight nine out of the ten battering-ships were on fire. The scene at this moment was awful beyond description, as the flames mounted higher and higher till they lighted up the whole bay and the surrounding shores. When it became evident that the ships could not be saved, there was a panic on board; all discipline was lost in the eagerness to escape from the burning decks; sailors and gunners threw themselves into the sea. French and Spanish boats picked up hundreds, and still there were hundreds more who were perishing, whose agonized shrieks rose upon the midnight air. The English heard it, and stout hearts that quailed not at the roar of guns, quivered

> " At the cry
> Of some strong swimmer in his agony."

Then it was that the English showed that their courage was equalled by their humanity, as the very men who had fought all day at the guns pushed off in boats to save their foes from drowning. This was an attempt which involved the utmost danger, for the ships were on fire, and might blow up at any moment. But Brigadier

Curtis, learning from the prisoners that hundreds of officers and men, some wounded, still remained on board, forgot everything in his eagerness to save them. Careless of danger from the explosions which every instant scattered fragments of wreck around him, he passed from ship to ship, and literally dragged from the burning decks the miserable Spaniards whom their own countrymen had left to perish. The Governor watched the movement with the utmost anxiety, which rose to "anguish," to use his own word, as he saw the gallant officer push his boat alongside one of the largest ships, that was a mass of flames. As he stood transfixed with horror at the sight, there came a tremendous explosion, and the ship was blown into the air, its fragments falling far and wide over the sea. That was a moment of agony, for he could not doubt that friend and foe had perished together. But as the wreck cleared away the little pinnace was seen, by the light of the other burning ships, to be still afloat, though shattered. A huge beam of timber had fallen through her flooring, killing the coxswain, wounding others of her crew, and starting a large hole in her bottom, through which the water rushed so rapidly that it seemed as if she must sink in a few minutes. But English sailors are equal to anything, and stripping off their jackets they stuffed them into the hole, and thus kept the boat above water till they reached the shore, bringing with them 357 of their late enemies, whom they had saved from a horrible death. The wounded were sent to the hospitals and treated with the greatest care; and an officer who died four days after, received the honors that would have been paid to one of their own countrymen, the grenadiers following his bier and firing their farewell shot

"O'er the grave where the hero was buried."

This last act was all that was wanting to complete the glory of England on that immortal day. History records the heroic conduct of British seamen at the Battle of the Nile, when the French Admiral's ship, the Orient, took fire, and Nelson sent his boats to pick up the drowning crew. While this should be remembered, let it not be forgotten that sixteen years before the Battle of the Nile, the garrison of Gibraltar had set the splendid example.

The next morning saw the bay covered with wrecks. The victory was complete. The siege was still kept up in form, and the besiegers continued firing, and for some days threw into the town four, five, and six hundred shells, and from six hundred to a thousand shot, every twenty-four hours! But this was only the muttering thunder after the storm. The battle was over, and from that day to this—more than a hundred years—the Red Cross of England has floated from the Rock of Gibraltar.

The close of this long and terrible conflict was like the ending of a play, when the curtain falls at last upon a scene of happy reunion. Even during the years of fiercest strife the courtesies of war had been strictly observed. Flags of truce passed between the garrison and the camp of the besiegers: prisoners were exchanged, and now and then one or the other of the commanders paid a compliment that was well deserved, to the courage and skill of his antagonist. Especially did the Duc de Crillon, true Frenchman as he was, indulge in these flattering phrases. In a letter written just before the attack of the battering-ships, he assures General Eliott of his "highest esteem," and of "the pleasure to which I look forward of becoming your friend, after I shall have proved myself worthy of the honor, by facing you as an enemy!" That pleasure he was now to have. He had faced the General as an enemy; he was now to know him as a friend.

For months, there had been whispers in the air of a coming peace, and the attitude of the contending parties was more that of armed neutrality than of active war.

At last the announcement came. The besiegers were the first to receive it, and sent the news to the garrison; but "Old Eliott," true soldier as he was, waited for orders from home. At length a British frigate sailed into the harbor with the blessed tidings that Great Britain had acknowledged the independence of America, and that the three powers—England, France, and Spain—had solemnly agreed to be at peace. Now all barriers to intercourse were removed, and the Governor rode out to meet his late enemy at a point midway between the lines. Both Generals instantly dismounted and embraced, thus answering a blow, or the many blows given and received, with a kiss. The Duke soon after returned the visit, and found the gates of Gibraltar, which had not been forced in three and a half years of war, now thrown wide open to his coming in the attitude of peace. He was received with all the honors of war. As he rode through the gates his appearance was greeted with loud huzzas, which ran along the lines, and echoed among the hills, a salutation which at first he did not understand, and was confused by it, as it might be interpreted as a cheer of triumph over a fallen enemy; but when it was explained to him that it was the way in which English soldiers greeted one whom they recognized as a hero, he was very much flattered by the demonstration. As the artillery officers were presented to him he complimented them highly on their courage and skill, saying pleasantly (no one could doubt his sincerity in this) that he "would rather see them here as friends than on their batteries as enemies!" And so at last, after these long and terrible years, the curtain fell on a scene as peaceful as ever ended a tragedy on the stage.

Such are the heroic memories which gather round Gibraltar, and overshadow it as its mighty crags cast their shadows on the sea. Let us not say, "All this is nothing to us, because we are neither Englishmen, nor Frenchmen, nor Spaniards." "We are men, and whatever concerns man concerns us." If it be indeed "beautiful to die for one's country," the spot is holy ground where, for the dear sake of "country," brave men have fought and died.

CHAPTER VIII.

THERE is one thing in Gibraltar which strikes me unpleasantly, and yet (such are the contradictions in our likes and dislikes) it is the very thing which has made it so attractive, viz., the English occupation. For picturesqueness of situation, the mighty Rock, standing at the entering in of the seas, is unique in the world, and the outlook along the shores of Africa and Europe is enough to captivate the eye of the most sight-worn traveller. And the people who hold this rock-fortress are worthy to be its masters, for they are not only brave, as soldiers are by profession, but they have all the manly qualities of the English race; they are chivalrous and generous. Nowhere does English hospitality appear more charming. If ever a man had occasion to like Gibraltar and the English in Gibraltar, I have; and I shall keep them both in grateful memory.

And yet—and yet—in this general accord of pleased reflection, which comes to me in the midst of these happy days, there is one thing which strikes a discordant note. The English are here, not by right of birth, but **of con-**

quest.   Gibraltar is not a part of England: it is a part of
Spain, to which it belongs by nature, if nature has anything to do with the boundaries of States.   True, the
English have taken it and hold it, and by the right of
war it belongs to them, as a fortress belongs to the power
that is strongest.   Yet that does not change the relation
of things, any more than it changes the geographical position of the captured fortress.   And so it remains that
England holds Gibraltar, I will not say in an enemy's
country, but certainly in a foreign country—a fact which,
however it be disguised, it is not pleasant to contemplate.

The stranger does not feel this so much while he is inside the gates as when he leaves the town and goes out
into the country.   Perhaps the reader will share my feeling if he will give me the pleasure of his company.   It
was a bright, crisp winter afternoon that a friend from
Boston and I planned an excursion on foot.   But stop a
moment!   When I travelled in the East I learned the
wisdom of the old Oriental custom of "girding up the
loins"; and so, stepping into a shop in Waterport Street,
I bought something like a soldier's belt, my only military
trapping, with which I braced myself so firmly together
that I felt "in prime marching order," and away we went
at a swinging gait, as merry as two New England boys
out of school and off for a holiday.   It is not a long walk
to the gates, and once through them and outside the walls
we took a long breath as we once more inhaled the free
air of the country.

At a little distance we came to a row of sentries—a line of red-coats that kept guard over the majesty of England. Then a half-mile walk across a low, sandy plain—the Neutral Ground—and we came to another line of sentinels in different uniforms and speaking a different tongue, a little beyond which is Linea (so named from its being just beyond the lines), a place of twelve thousand inhabitants, which has the three requisites of a Spanish town—a church, a market, and a bull-ring!

Here was the situation: a double line of soldiers facing each other, not in a hostile attitude, not training their guns on each other, but certainly not in a position which was calculated to promote friendly relations.

Strolling through the town it seemed to us (perhaps it was only imagination) that there was a sullen look in the faces of the people; that they did not regard Englishmen, or those speaking the English tongue, with special affection. Linea has a bad name for being a nest of smugglers; but whether it is worse than other frontier towns, which afford special facilities for smuggling, and therefore offer great temptations, I cannot say. It was not an attractive place, and after an hour's walk we retraced our steps back to our fortress home.

As we turned toward the Rock we were facing the British Lion just as the descending sun was putting a crown upon his royal head. Never did he wear a more kingly look than in that evening sky. If the God of War has a throne on earth, it must be on that height, more than a thousand feet in air, looking down on the petty human creatures below, all of whom he could destroy with one breath of his nostrils.

It was indeed a glorious sight. But how do the Spaniards like it? How should *we* like it if we were in their place? This was a very inconvenient question to be asked just at that moment, as we were crossing the Neutral Ground. But if I *must* answer, I cannot but say that, if I were a Spanish sentinel, pacing back and forth in such a presence and compelled at every turn to look up at that Lion frowning over me, it would be with a very bitter feeling. I might even ask my English friends who are masters of Gibraltar, how they would like to see the flag of another country floating over a part of *their* country?

Of course, the retention of Gibraltar is to England a matter of pride. It is a great thing to see the red cross flying on the top of the Rock in the sight of two continents, and of all who go sailing up and down in these waters. But this pride has to be paid for by a good many entanglements of one kind and another.

For example: It is a constant source of complaint on the part of Spain that Gibraltar is the headquarters for smuggling across the frontier. This is not at all surprising, since (like Singapore and perhaps other distant places in the British Empire) it is a "free port." Its deliverance from commercial restrictions dates back to the reign of Queen Anne, in the beginning of the last century—an im-

8

munity which it has enjoyed for nearly two hundred years. A few years since a light restriction was placed upon wines and spirits, probably for a moral rather than a commercial purpose, lest their too great abundance might lead to drunkenness among the soldiers. But with respect to everything else used by man, trade is absolutely free; whatever is brought here for sale is not burdened with the added tax of an import duty. Though Gibraltar is so near Tarifa, there is no *tariff* levied on merchandise any more than on voyagers that go up and down the seas. Not only English goods, but French and Italian goods, all are free; even those which, if imported into England, would pay duty, here pay none, so that they are cheaper than in England itself. Thus Gibraltar is the paradise of free-traders, since in it there is no such " accursed thing " as a custom-house, and no such hated official as a custom-house officer! This puts it at an advantage as compared with any port or city or country which is not free, and they have to suffer from the difference. Especially does Spain, which is not yet converted to free trade, suffer from its close contact with its more liberal neighbor. The extraordinary cheapness on one side of the Neutral Ground, as compared with the dearness on the other, is a temptation to smuggling which it requires more virtue than the Spaniards possess to resist.

The temptation takes them on their weakest side when it presents itself in the form of tobacco, for the Spaniards are a nation of smokers. The manufacture and sale of tobacco is a monopoly of the Government, and yields a large revenue, amounting, I believe, to fifteen millions of dollars. It might amount to twice as much if every smoker in Spain bought only Spanish tobacco. But who will pay the price for the Government cigars and cigarettes when they can be obtained without paying duty? Smuggling is going on every day, and every hour of the day; and the Spaniards say that it is winked at and encouraged by the English in Gibraltar; to which the latter reply that whatever smuggling is done, is done by the Spaniards themselves, for which they are not responsible. A shopkeeper in Gibraltar has as good a right to sell a pound of tobacco to a Spanish peasant as to an English sailor. What becomes of it after it leaves his shop is no concern of his. Of course the Spanish police are numerous, and are, or are supposed to be, vigilant. The Carabineros are stationed at the lines, whose duty it is to keep a sharp look-out on every passing vehicle; whether it be a lordly carriage rolling swiftly by, or a market wagon; to poke their noses into every little cart; to lift up the panniers of every donkey; and even to thrust their hands into every basket, and to give a pinch to every suspicious-looking parcel. And yet, with this great display of watchfulness, which indeed is a little overdone, somehow an immense quantity slips through their fingers. Many amusing stories are told of contrabandists. One honest Spaniard had a wonderful dog that went through miraculous transformations: he was sometimes fat and sometimes lean, nature (or man) having provided him with a double skin, between which was packed a handsome allowance of tobacco. This dog was a model of docility, and would play with other dogs, like the poor innocent that he was, and then dart off to his master to "unload" and be sent back again! It was said that he would make several trips a day. In another case a poor man tried to make an honest living by raising turkeys for market; but even then fate had a spite against him, for after he had brought them into town, he had no luck in selling them! The same ill-fortune attended him every day. But one evening, as he came out of the gates looking sad and sorrowful, the Carabineros took a closer inspection of his cart, and found that every turkey had been prepared for another market than that of Gibraltar, by a well-spiced "stuffing" under her motherly wings!

Of course the Spanish officers are indignant at the duplicity which permits this smuggling to take place, and utter great oaths in sonorous Castilian against their treacherous neighbors. But even the guardians of the law may fall from virtue. The Governor, who took office here but a few weeks since, tells me that when the Governor of Algeciras, the Spanish town across the bay, came to pay his respects to him, the officers of his suite, while their horses were standing in the court of the Convent [the Government House], filled their pockets with tobacco! Fit agents indeed to collect the revenue of Spain!

But smuggling is not the worst of the complications that arise out of having a fortress in a foreign country. Another is that Gibraltar becomes the resort of all the characters that find Spain too hot to hold them. Men who have committed offences against Spanish law, flee across the lines and claim protection. Some of them are political refugees, who have escaped from a Government that would persecute and perhaps imprison them for their opinions, and find safety under the English flag. The necessity for this protection is not so great now as in former years, when the Government of Spain was a despotism as absolute and intolerant as any in Europe. Even so late as thirty years ago, Castelar would have been shot if he had not escaped across the frontier into Switzerland; as his father, twenty years before, had been sentenced to death, and would have been executed if he had not made haste to get inside of Gibraltar, and remained here seven years. In his case, as in many others, the old fortress was a bulwark against tyranny. Within these walls the laws of national hospitality were sacred. No Spanish patriot could be taken from under this flag, to be sent to the dungeon or the scaffold. All honor to England, that she has a City of Refuge for the free and the brave of all lands, and that she has so often sheltered and saved those who were the champions, and but for her would have been the martyrs, of liberty!

But the greater number of those who seek a refuge here have no claim to protection, since they are not

political refugees, but ordinary criminals—thieves, and
sometimes murderers—who have fled here to escape the
punishment of their crimes. In such cases it is easy
to say what should be done with them: they should be
given up at once to the Spanish authorities, to be tried
by Spanish law and receive the just reward of their
deeds.

If all cases were like these, the disposition of them
would be a very simple matter. But they are not all so
clear; some of them, indeed, are very complex, involving
questions of international law, which an army officer, or
even a civil officer, might not understand. A man may
be accused of crime by the Spanish authorities, and yet,
in the eye of impartial judges of another country, be
guilty of no greater crime than loving his country too
well. But the Spanish Government demands his surrender. The case is referred to the Colonial Secretary, as
the highest authority in Gibraltar next to the Governor.
It is a grave responsibility, which requires not only a disposition to do what is right and just, but a knowledge of
law which a military or a civil officer may not possess.
The present Secretary is Lord Gifford, and a more honorable English gentleman it would be impossible to find.
But though a gallant soldier, brave and accomplished as
he is, he may not be familiar with all the points which he
may have to decide. He tells me that this matter of extradition is the most difficult duty that is laid upon him.
He said, "I have two cases before me to-day," in the de-

cision of which he seemed a good deal perplexed. With
the most earnest desire to decide right, he might decide
wrong.   His predecessor had been removed for extradit-
ing a man without proper authority.   He told me the incident to illustrate the responsibility of his position, and
the extreme difficulty of adjudicating cases which are of a
doubtful character.   It was this: The island of Cuba, as
Americans know too well, is in a chronic state of insurrection.   In one of the numerous outbreaks, a man who
was implicated made his escape, and took refuge in Tangier, and while there asked of some visitors from Gibraltar if he would be safe here, to which they promptly replied, "Certainly ; that he could not be given up," and
on the strength of that assurance he came ; but the Spanish agents were watching, and somehow managed to influence the officers here to surrender him.   The English
Government promptly disavowed the act, and claimed
that the man was still under their protection, and should
be brought back.   This Spanish pride did not permit
them to do.   However, he was sent to Port Mahon, in
the Balearic Islands, and there (perhaps by the conniv-
ance of the authorities, who may have thought it the
easiest way to get rid of a troublesome question) he was
not so closely guarded but that he was able to make his
escape, and so the matter ended.   But the Colonial Secretary who had permitted his extradition was promptly recalled, in disapprobation of his conduct.   With such a
warning before him, as well as from his own desire to do

justice, the present Secretary wished to act with due prudence and caution, that he might not share the fate of his predecessor. I could but admire his patience and care, and yet a stranger can but reflect that all this complication and embarrassment comes from holding a fortress in a foreign country!

But while this is true, yet what are such petty vexations as smuggling and extradition; what is the million of dollars a year which it costs to keep Gibraltar; in a matter which concerns the majesty and the colossal pride of England—the sense of power to hold her own against the world? A hundred years ago Burke spoke of Gibraltar with exultation as "a post of power, a post of superiority, of connection, of commerce—one which makes us invaluable to our friends and dreadful to our enemies;" and the feeling has survived to this day. Not an Englishman passes through the Straits whose heart does not swell within him to see the flag of his country floating from the top of the Rock, from which, as he believes, the whole world cannot tear it down. Every true Briton would look upon the lowering of that flag as the abdication of Imperial power.

But is not this an over-estimate of the value of Gibraltar to England? Is it worth all it costs? Would it weigh much in the balance in a great contest of nations for the mastery of the world? The object of this Rock-fortress is to command the passage into the Mediterranean. The arms of Gibraltar are a Castle and a Key, to signify that it holds the key of the Straits, and that no ship flying any other flag than that of England can enter or depart except by her permission. But that power is already gone. England may hold the key of the Straits, but the door is too wide to be bolted. The hundred-ton guns of Gibraltar, even if aimed directly seaward, could not destroy or stop a passing fleet. I know this is not the limit of construction in modern ordnance. Guns have been wrought weighing a hundred and twenty tons, which throw a ball weighing a ton over ten miles! Such a gun mounted at Tarifa might indeed hurl its tremendous bolt across the Mediterranean into Africa. But Tarifa is in Spain, while opposite Gibraltar it is fourteen miles to Ceuta, a point not to be reached by any ordnance in existence, even if the last product of modern warfare were mounted on the height of O'Hara's Tower; so that a fleet of ironclads, hugging the African coast, would be quite safe from the English fire, which could not prevent the entrance of a French or German or Russian fleet into the Mediterranean, if it were strong enough to encounter the English fleet.

The reliance must be therefore on the fleet, not on the fortress. Of course the latter would be a refuge in case of disaster, where the English ships could find protection under the guns of the fort. But the fortress *alone* could not bar the passage into the Mediterranean.

As to the fleet, England has been mistress of the seas for more than a century; and yet it does not follow that

she will always retain this supremacy. Her fleet is still
the largest and most powerful in the world, and her seamen as skilful and as brave as in the days of Nelson; but
the conditions of naval warfare are greatly changed. The
use of steam for ships of war as well as for commerce, and
the building of ironclads mounted with enormous guns,
tend to equalize the conditions of war. Battles may be
decided by the weight of guns or the thickness of defen-
sive armor, and in these particulars other nations have advanced as well as England. France, Germany, and Russia
have vied with each other as to which should build the
most tremendous ships of war. Even Italy has within a
few years risen to the rank of a first-class naval power, as
she has some of the largest ships in the world. The
Italia, which I saw lying in the harbor of Naples, could
probably have destroyed the whole fleet with which Nelson won the battle of Trafalgar; and hence the Italian
fleet must be counted as a factor of no second importance
in any future struggle for the control of the Mediterranean.

And yet some military authorities think too much importance is attached to these modern inventions. Farragut did not believe in iron ships. He judged from his
own experience in naval warfare, and no man had had
greater. He had found wooden ships good enough to win
his splendid victories. In his famous attack upon Mobile
he ran his fleet close under the guns of the fort, himself
standing in the round-top of his flag-ship to overlook the

whole scene of battle, and then boldly attacked ironclads, and sunk them in the open bay. His motto was: "Wooden ships and iron hearts!" Ships and guns are good, but men are better. And so I do not give up my faith in English prowess and skill, but hold that, whatever the improvements in ships or guns, to the last hour that men meet each other face to face in battle, the issue will depend largely on a genius in war; on the daring to seize unexpected opportunities; to take advantage of sudden changes; and thus by some master-stroke to turn what seemed inevitable defeat into victory.

In the year 1867 I crossed the Atlantic in the Great Eastern, then in command of Sir James Anderson. Among the passengers was the Austrian Admiral Tegetthoff, who had the year before gained the battle of Lissa, with whom I formed a pleasant acquaintance; and as we walked the deck together, drew from him some particulars of that great victory. He was as modest as he was brave, and did not like to talk of himself; but in answer to my inquiries, said that before the battle he knew the immense superiority of the Italian fleet; and that his only hope of victory was in disregarding all the ordinary rules of naval warfare: that, instead of drawing up his ships in the usual line of battle, he must rush into the centre of the enemy, and confuse them by the suddenness of his attack where they did not expect him. The manœuvre was successful even beyond his own expectation. The *Rè d' Italia*, the flagship of the Italian Admiral, which had

been built in New York as the masterpiece of naval archi-
tecture, was sunk, and the fleet utterly defeated! What
Tegetthoff did at Lissa, the English may do in future
battles. Of this I am sure, that whatever *can* be done by
courage and skill will be done by the sons of the Vikings
to retain their mastery of the sea. But it would be too
much to expect of any power that it could stand against
the combined navies of the world.

If Gibraltar be thus powerless for offence, is it altogether secure for defence? Is it really impregnable?
That is a question often asked, and on which only military men are competent to give an opinion, and even they
are divided. Englishmen, who are most familiar with its
defences, say, Yes! Those defences have been enormous-
ly increased even in our day. In the Great Siege we saw
its powers of resistance a hundred years ago. Yet Eliott
defeated the French and Spanish fleets and armies with
less than a hundred guns. Ninety years later—in 1870—
there were *seven hundred* guns in position on the Rock,
the smallest of which were larger than the heaviest
used in the siege. And yet since 1870 the increase in
the size of guns and their weight of metal, is greater than
in the hundred years before. In the siege it was counted
a wonderful shot that carried a ball two miles and a half.
Now the hundred-ton guns carry over eight miles. Putting
these things together, English officers maintain that Gibraltar cannot be taken by all the powers of Europe combined.

On the other hand, French and German engineers—familiar with the new inventions in war, and knowing that they can use dynamite and nitro-glycerine, instead of gunpowder, to give tremendous force to the new projectiles—would probably say that there is no fortress which cannot be battered down.   To me, who am but a layman in such matters, as I walk about Gibraltar, it seems that, if all the armies of Europe should come up against it, they could make no impression on its rock-ribbed sides; that only some convulsion of nature could shake its "everlasting foundations."   And yet such is the power of modern explosives to rend the rocks and hills, with a new invention every year of something still more terrible, that we know not but they may at last almost tear the solid globe asunder.   What wreck and ruin of the works of man may be wrought by such engines of destruction, it is not given us to foresee.

Meanwhile to the Spaniards the English possession of Gibraltar is a constant irritation.   It is of no use to remind them that they had it once, and might have kept it; that is no comfort; it only makes the matter worse; for they are like spoiled children, who grieve the most for that which they have thrown away.   Again it was offered to them by England, with only the condition that they should not sell Florida to Napoleon; but as he was then in the height of his career, they thought it safer to trust to his protection; albeit a few years later they found out his treachery, and had to depend on an English army, led

by Wellington, to drive the French out of Spain. And
still these spoiled children of the South will not recognize
the English sovereignty. To this day the King of Spain
claims Gibraltar as a part of his dominions, though he
recognizes it as " temporarily in the possession of the
English," and all who are born on the Rock are entitled
to the rights of Spanish subjects !

But whether Gibraltar can be " taken " or not by siege
or storm, in the course of human events there may be a
turn of fortune which shall compel England to surrender
it. If there should come a general European war, in
which there should be (what the first Napoleon endeavored to effect) a combination of all the Continental
powers against England, she might, standing alone, be
reduced to such extremity as to be obliged to sue for
peace, and one of the hard conditions forced upon her
might be the surrender of Gibraltar !

But while we may speculate on such a possibility of
the future, it is not a change which I desire to see in my
day. The transfer of Gibraltar to Spain might satisfy
Spanish pride, but I fear that it would be no longer what
it is if it had not the treasury of England to supply its
numerous wants. The Spaniards are not good managers,
and Gibraltar would ere long sink into the condition of an
old, decayed Spanish town. Further than this, I confess
that, as a matter of sentiment, it would be no pleasure to
me to visit it if the charm of its present society were
gone. I should miss greatly the English faces, so manly

and yet so kindly, and the dear old mother tongue.   So while I live I hope Gibraltar will be held by English soldiers.   "After me the deluge!"

No: not the deluge, but universal peace!   Let the old Rock remain as it is.   Lover of peace as I am, I should be sorry to see it dismantled.   It would not be the same thing if it were to become another Capri—a mere resort for artists, who should sit upon Europa Point, and make their sketches; or if lovers only should saunter in the Alameda gardens, whispering softly as they look out upon the moonlit sea.   The mighty crag that bears the name of Hercules should bear on its front something which speaks of power.   Let the Great Fortress remain as the grim monument of War, even when men learn war no more; as the castles on the Rhine are kept as the monuments of mediæval barbarism.   If its guns are all silent, or unshotted, it will stand for something more than a symbol of brute force: it will be a monumental proof that the blessed age of peace has come.   Then, if there be any change in the flag that waves over it; if the Red Cross of England, which has never been lowered in war, should give place to an emblem of universal peace; it may be a Red Cross still—red in sign of blood, but only of that blood which was shed alike for all nations, and which is yet to unite in One Brotherhood the whole Family of Mankind.

CHAPTER IX.

FAREWELL TO GIBRALTAR—LEAVING FOR AFRICA.

ALL too swiftly the days flew by, and the time of my visit to Gibraltar was coming to an end. But in travel I have often found that the last taste was the sweetest. It is only when you have come to know a place well that you can fully enjoy it; when emancipated from guides, with no self-appointed cicerone to dog your footsteps and intrude his stereotyped observations; when, in short, you have obtained "the freedom of the place" by right of familiar acquaintance, and can wander about alone, sauntering slowly in favorite walks, or sitting under the shade of the trees, and looking off upon the purple mountains or the rippling sea, that you are fully master of the situation. "Days of idleness," as they are called, are sometimes, of all days, at once the busiest and the happiest, when, having finished up all regular and routine work, and thus done his duty as a traveller, one devotes himself to "odds and ends," and gathers up his varied impressions into one delightful whole. These are delicious moments, when the pleasure of a foreign clime—

"Blest be the time, the clime, the spot!"—

becomes so intense that we are reluctant to let it go, and
linger still, clinging to that which is nearly exhausted, as
if we would drain the cup to the very last drop.

Such is the feeling that comes in these last days, as I
go wandering about, full of moods and fancies born of
the place and the hour. There is a strange spell and fas-
cination in the Rock itself. If it be proper ever to speak
of respect for inanimate things, next to a great mountain,
I have a profound respect for a great rock. It is the emblem of strength and power, which by its very height
shelters and protects the feebleness of man. How often
on the desert, under the burning sun, have I espied afar
off a huge cliff rising above the plain, and urging on my
wearied camel, thrown myself from it, and found the in-
expressible relief of "the shadow of a great rock in a
weary land!" So here this mountain wall that rises
above me, does not awe and overwhelm so much as it
shelters and protects; the higher it lifts its head, the
more it carries me upward, and gives me an outlook
over a wider horizon. If I were a dweller in Gibraltar,
I would seek out every sequestered nook upon its side,
where I could be away from the haunts of men, and
could "dream dreams and see visions." Often would I
climb to the Signal Station, or O'Hara's Tower, to see
the glory of the sunrisings and sunsettings; and, as the
evening comes on, to see the African mountains cast-
ing their shadows over the broad line of coast and the
broader sea.

9

Next to the Rock itself, the oldest thing in Gibraltar—the very oldest that man has made—is the Moorish Castle, on which the Moslem invader planted the standard of the Crescent near twelve centuries ago, making this his first stronghold in the land which he was to conquer. And now I must look upon its face again, because of its very age. American as I am, coming from a country where everything is supposed to be " brand new," I feel a strange delight in these old castles and towers, and even in ruins, gray with the moss of centuries. I know it is a "far cry" to the time of the Moors, but we must not think of it as a time of barbarism. The period in which the Moors held Gibraltar was that of the Moorish rule in Spain, when they were the most highly civilized people in Europe, and the Goths were the barbarians. In that day the old Moorish town must have been a very picturesque place, with the domes of its mosques, and the slender minarets rising above them, from which at the sunset hour voices called the faithful to prayer ; and very picturesque figures were those of the turbaned Moors, as they reverently turned toward Mecca, and bowed themselves and worshipped.

Nor did the romance die when the Spaniards followed in the procession of races, for they were only less picturesque than the Moors. They too had their good times. A life which would seem tame and dull to the modern Englishman had its charms for the children of the sun, whether they were children of Europe or of Africa.

When the church took the place of the mosque, mollahs and ulemas were replaced by priests and monks; and the old Franciscan friars, whose Convent is now the residence of the Governor, marched in sombre procession through the streets, and instead of the call from the minaret, the evening was made holy by the sound of the Ave Maria or the Angelus bell. And these Spaniards had their gayeties as well as their solemnities. They danced as well as prayed. When their prayers were ended, the same dark-eyed senoritas who had knelt in the churches sat on balconies in the moonlight, while gallant cavaliers sang their songs and tinkled their guitars—diversions which filled the intervals of stern and savage war. Out of all this strange old history, with many a heroic episode that still lives in Spanish song and story, might be wrought, if there were another Irving to tell the tale, an historical romance as fascinating as that of the Conquest of Granada. The materials are abundant; all that is wanting is that they be touched by the wand of the enchanter.

But as I have just now more freshly in mind the English history of Gibraltar, I leave the Spaniards and the Moors, and betake me to the King's Bastion, on which "Old Eliott" stood on the greatest day that Gibraltar ever saw. And here we must not forget the second in command, his brave companion-in-arms, General Boyd, who built the Bastion in 1773, and who, on laying the first stone, prayed "that he might live to see it resist the united fleets of France and Spain"—a wish that was

gloriously fulfilled nine years later, when he took part in
the immortal defence; and it is fitting that his body
should sleep under his own work, at once the instrument
and the monument of that great victory. Even the trees
have a historic air, as they are old—at least many of them
have a look of age. One would think that the constant
firing of guns, the shock and "sulphurous canopy," would
kill vegetation or stunt it in its growth. But there are
many fine old trees in Gibraltar. Near the Alameda
stands a magnificent *bella sombra* (so named because its
wide-spreading branches are dark and sombre, and yet
strangely beautiful), which must be very old. Perhaps it
was standing a century ago, and heard all the guns fired
in the Great Siege, as possibly a few years later it may
have heard, across the bay and away over the Spanish
hills, even the thunder of Nelson at Trafalgar.

On one of the last days I had engaged to take a midday
dinner with the pastor of the Scotch Church, who lives in
the southern part of the town. It is a pleasant walk beyond the Alameda over the hill, where you can but stop
now and then to look down on the long breakwater of the
New Mole, or into the quiet dock of Rosia Bay; or to
hear the bugles waken the echoes of the hills. After
dinner my friend proposed a stroll, in which I was glad
to join him, especially as it took me to new points of
view, from which I could look up at the Rock on its
southern side, as I had already seen it on the north.
Taking our way across the level plateau of Windmill

WINDMILL HILL AND O'HARA'S TOWER.

Hill, past barracks and hospitals that are here somewhat retired from the shore, we descended toward the sea.

This end of Gibraltar is a great resort of the people in the summer time, and furnishes the only drive, unless they go out of the gates and crossing the Neutral Ground enter the Spanish lines. Here they are wholly within the Peninsula, and yet in a space so limited is a drive such as one might find along the Riviera. The road is beautifully kept, and winds in and out among the rocks, in one place crossing a deep gorge, which makes you almost dizzy as you look over the parapet of the little bridge which spans it. At each turn you get some new glimpse of the sea, and whenever you raise your eyes to look across the Strait, there is the long line of the African Coast. This is the favorite drive of officers and ladies on summer afternoons, since here they can escape the blistering sun, and get into the cool shadows.

As we come to Europa Point we are at the very foot of the Rock, and must stop to look upward; for above us rises the highest point of Gibraltar, O'Hara's Tower, which, as it is also nearest to the sea, is the one that first catches the eye of the mariner sailing up or down the Mediterranean. Here the old Phœnicians sacrificed to Hercules, as they were approaching what was to them the end of the habitable globe; and here, in later ages. a lamp was always hung before the shrine of the Virgin, and the devout sailor crossed himself and repeated his Ave Maria as he floated by.

Winding round Europa Point, we found our progress
barred by an iron gateway; but rattling at the gate
brought a sentinel, who, seeing nothing suspicious in our
appearance, allowed us to enter the guarded enclosure.
Here in this quiet spot, on a shelf of rock which hangs
above the road, and is itself overhung by the mighty clift
which rises behind it and above it, is the cottage which
is the Governor's summer retreat. The Convent answers
very well for a winter residence; but in summer Gibraltar is a very hot place, as it has the reflection of the
sun both from the sea in front and the Rock behind; and
the Convent, standing on the shore of the bay, gets the
full force of both. But there are cool retreats both north
and south. On the north the townsfolk pour out of the
gates to get under the giant cliff which casts its mighty
shadow across the Neutral Ground. A little farther to
the east, they come to the sands of a beach, which seems
so like a watering-place in dear Old England that they
have christened it Margate. So also, turning the corner
at the south end of the Rock, one is sheltered from the
heat in the long summer afternoon. The cottage is without any pretension to ornament; but as it has a somewhat elevated perch, like a Swiss chalet, it is a sort of
eyrie, in which one can look down upon the sea and catch
every wind that comes from the Mediterranean.

Just now this little eyrie was turned to another purpose
—as a place of confinement for Zebehr Pasha, a name
that brings back memories of Egypt. An Arab sheikh,

at the head of one of the most powerful tribes on the
Upper Nile, he was at the same time one of the most
famous slave-hunters of Africa. And yet such was his
influence in the Soudan, that he was the one man to
whom Gordon turned in his isolation at Khartoum, when
neither England nor Egypt came to the rescue; and his
one message to the authorities at Cairo was: "Send me
Zebehr Pasha!" The request was refused, and we know
the rest. Had it been granted, the result might have
been different. But the British Government seemed to
have a great fear of letting him return to the scene of his
old exploits lest he should turn against them, and after
the English occupation of Egypt, had him remanded for
safe-keeping to Gibraltar. His detention is made as little irksome as possible. He is not confined in a prison.
He is even the occupant of the Governor's cottage, and
has his family with him. Looking up at the windows, I
saw dark faces (perhaps those of his wives), that moved
away as soon as they were observed. But to be comfort-
ably housed is nothing without liberty. To the lion in
captivity it matters little whether he is in a barred cage,
or has the most luxurious quarters in a Royal Zoölogical
Garden. Zebehr Pasha is a lion of the desert that has
never been tamed. How he must chafe at the gilded
bars of his prison, and look out wistfully upon the blue
waves that separate him from his beloved Africa! He
envies the eagles that he sees soaring and screaming over
the sea. If they would but lend him their wings, he

would "homeward fly," and mounting the swiftest drome-
dary, taste once more the wild freedom of the desert.*

But all things must have an end, and my stay in Gibraltar, delightful as it was, must be brought to a close. I
was not eager to depart. So quickly does one become
at home in new surroundings, that a place which I never
saw till a few days before, now seemed like an old
friend. My new acquaintances said I "ought to stay a
month at least," and I was sure that it would pass quickly
and delightfully. But travellers, like city tramps, must
" move on," and it is certainly better to go regretting and
regretted, than to carry away only disagreeable memories.
I had taken passage for Oran on the Barbary Coast, when
the Colonial Secretary, kind to the last, proposed to send
me off to the ship in a government launch, an offer which
my modesty compelled me to decline. But he insisted
(for these Englishmen, when they do a thing, must do it

---

* A few months after I left Gibraltar, the old Arab was set at liberty by
the British Government, but on very strict conditions. A letter from the
American Consul, in reply to my questions, says:

"Zebehr Pasha was released August 3, 1887, on signing a certain docu-
ment sent from the Home Government relative to his future conduct. This
was an engagement 'to remain in the place which should be chosen by the
Egyptian Government; to place himself under its surveillance; and to ab-
stain from interference in political or military questions relating to the Soudan or otherwise.' This he signed in the presence of two British staff officers.
He had arrived in Gibraltar in March, 1885, and from that time had been a
prisoner in the Governor's cottage for about two years and a half, under
charge at different times of several officers of the garrison. He left Gibraltar
August 16th, for Port Said, accompanied by his household, which included
two women and three men, and was attended by three male and two female
servants. He also took back to his African home an infant born in the
Governor's cottage at Europa."

handsomely) till I had to submit. That evening, while dining at the Hotel, a servant brought me word that a messenger had a special message for me, and when I presented myself, he put into my hands the following:

"*Memorandum from the Colonial Secretary*
                              to the Captain of the Port.

"Dr. Field, an American gentleman, introduced here by Sir Clare Ford, is now staying at the Royal Hotel, and leaving Friday evening by the steamer for Algiers.

"His Excellency wishes every attention to be shown him: so you will send a Boarding Officer to-morrow at 6 P. M., and ask him at what hour he desires to leave from Waterport, and have a launch ready for him: the Boarding Officer making all arrangements for Dr. Field and his friends passing through the gates.

                                        GIFFORD."

On the back of the above order was written in red ink, in very large letters:

"BOARDING OFFICER: *Comply with His Excellency's wishes.*
                              "G. B. BASSADONE,
                                  "For the Captain of the Port."

This was the first time in my life that I had been waited upon for orders! Having this greatness thrust upon me, I did not betray my unfamiliarity with such things by any light and trivial conduct, but kept my dignity with a sober face, and graciously announced my sovereign pleasure to depart the following evening at eight o'clock. This was really a great convenience, as it gave me a few hours more on shore, whereas otherwise I must leave be-

fore sunset, when the gates are shut, not to be opened till
morning. Appreciating not only the courtesy, but the
distinction, I invited an American party at the Hotel to
keep me company. But they had already made their arrangements, and went off ingloriously before "gun-fire";
while His Republican Highness took his dinner quietly,
and awaited the coming of his escort. One young lady,
however, (a cousin of Mr. Joseph H. Choate, of New York,
my friend and neighbor at our summer homes in the
Berkshire Hills,) stood by me, and at eight o'clock in the
evening we walked down Waterport Street, attended by
two stalwart defenders. The street was strangely silent,
for as the outsiders leave at sunset when the gates are
closed, the town is very quiet. It was dark as we approached the first gate, which had been shut hours before; but the guard, having "received orders," instantly
appeared to unlock it, a form which was repeated at the
second line of fortifications. At the quay we found the
launch ready, with steam up, and as we took our places
in the stern of the boat, on the cushioned seat provided
for distinguished guests, I felt as if I were a Lord High
Admiral. It was a beautiful night. The moon was up,
though half hidden by clouds, from which now and then
she burst forth, covering the bay with a flood of light.
At that moment—stern Puritan as I am, and impassible
as my friends know me to be—if I had been put upon
my oath, or my honor, I should have been compelled to
confess, that to be floating over a moonlit sea, with a fair

EUROPA POINT

countrywoman at my side, was not altogether the most
miserable position in which I have ever been placed in my
wanderings up and down in this world.

Once on the deck, the whole broadside of the Rock was
before us, with the lights glimmering far up and down
the heights. At half-past nine the last gun was fired,
and in another half hour the lights in the barracks were
put out, and all was dark and still.

It was midnight when the steamer began to move.
The moon had now flung off her misty veil, and risen to
the zenith, where she hung over the very crest of the
Rock, her soft light falling on every projecting crag. The
ship itself seemed to feel the holy stillness of the night,
and glided like a phantom-ship, almost without a sound,
over the unruffled sea. As we crept past the long line of
batteries, the great Fortress, with its hundreds of guns,
was silent; the Lion was sleeping, with all his thunders
muffled in his rocky breast. Thus our last glimpse of
Gibraltar was a vision not of War, but of Peace, as we
rounded Europa Point and set our faces toward Africa.

www.ingramcontent.com/pod-product-compliance
Lightning Source LLC
Chambersburg PA
CBHW030900050726
47500CB00009B/473